WordPress

FOR SMALL BUSINESS

EASY STRATEGIES TO BUILD A DYNAMIC WEBSITE WITH WORDPRESS

Scott Wilson

TYCHO
PRESS

Copyright © 2015 by Tycho Press, Berkeley, California

No part of this publication may be reproduced, stored in a retrieval system or transmitted in any form or by any means, electronic, mechanical, photocopying, recording, scanning or otherwise, except as permitted under Sections 107 or 108 of the 1976 United States Copyright Act, without the prior written permission of the Publisher. Requests to the Publisher for permission should be addressed to the Permissions Department, Tycho Press, 918 Parker St, Suite A-12, Berkeley, CA 94710.

Limit of Liability/Disclaimer of Warranty: The Publisher and the author make no representations or warranties with respect to the accuracy or completeness of the contents of this work and specifically disclaim all warranties, including without limitation warranties of fitness for a particular purpose. No warranty may be created or extended by sales or promotional materials. The advice and strategies contained herein may not be suitable for every situation. This work is sold with the understanding that the publisher is not engaged in rendering medical, legal or other professional advice or services. If professional assistance is required, the services of a competent professional person should be sought. Neither the Publisher nor the author shall be liable for damages arising herefrom. The fact that an individual, organization or website is referred to in this work as a citation and/or potential source of further information does not mean that the author or the Publisher endorses the information the individual, organization or website may provide or recommendations they/it may make. Further, readers should be aware that Internet websites listed in this work may have changed or disappeared between when this work was written and when it is read.

This book is in no way authorized by, endorsed by, or affiliated with WordPress® or its subsidiaries. All references to WordPress® and other trademarked properties are used in accordance with the Fair Use Doctrine and are not meant to imply that this book is a WordPress® product for advertising or other commercial purposes.

For general information on our other products and services or to obtain technical support, please contact our Customer Care Department within the U.S. at (866) 744-2665, or outside the U.S. at (510) 253-0500.

Tycho Press publishes its books in a variety of electronic and print formats. Some content that appears in print may not be available in electronic books, and vice versa.

TRADEMARKS: Tycho Press and the Tycho Press logo are trademarks or registered trademarks of Callisto Media Inc. and/or its affiliates, in the United States and other countries, and may not be used without written permission. All other trademarks are the property of their respective owners. Tycho Press is not associated with any product or vendor mentioned in this book.

ISBN: Print 978-1-62315-627-5 | eBook 978-1-62315-633-6

WORDPRESS

FOR SMALL BUSINESS

DISCARD

DID YOU KNOW?

409 million people view WordPress web-sites **each month.**

WordPress serves up **more than 17.6 billion pages each month.**

61 million new posts and **56 million new comments** are created on WordPress **each month.**

CNN, UPS, eBay, and the **NFL** all use WordPress.

WordPress powers nearly **a quarter of all websites on the Internet.**

WordPress software has been downloaded more than **150 million times** and runs more than **15 million websites.**

WordCamp, the conference that focuses on everything WordPress-related, has been held **over 350 times in over 150 cities around the world.**

CONTENTS

PART 1
What WordPress Can Do for You 7

Small Business in a Big Online World 8
A Range of Possibilities 11
Setting Your Goals 18

PART 2
Your WordPress Site 25

Build a Home 26
Lay It Out 34
Add Features 39
Get Organized 47
Be Easy to Find 53
Create Content 63
Get Paid 70

PART 3
Going Public 79

Interact 80
Make Friends 85
Measure Your Success 90
Stay Safe 98

Glossary 106

Resources 108

Index 112

PART

1

WHAT WORDPRESS CAN DO FOR YOU

You might be brand new to WordPress, but you definitely know your own business inside and out. You know your product, you know your customers, and you know what they want from you. Compared to that, learning WordPress is easy. So let's get started.

SMALL BUSINESS IN A BIG ONLINE WORLD

FIGURE 1 Many well-known websites run on WordPress.

Once upon a time, if you were the first bakery in town to have a website, you were hip, distinctive, and cool. You stood out. People in town looking for baked goods on the Internet—not that there were very many of them, but still—surely ran across your site. You got buzz. You led the trend.

Now every bakery has a website. If yours doesn't have one, you're behind the times. (Eventually, *not* having a website will probably become cool, but not just yet.) Even if you do have a site, it doesn't cause buzz—it's not cool, it's *expected*, and there's probably nothing that makes your site stand out from the crowd. Your site might as well be one of a million different sugar cookies, all created with the same cookie cutter.

With the proliferation of commerce on the Internet, online opportunities have also exploded. Tablets, smartphones, ubiquitous wireless access, a wealth of reference materials and information at our fingertips—these things all combine to create two things:

- For consumers, the expectation that any business worth buying from can be found somewhere on the Web.
- For businesses, the desire to get all those potential customers to buy from them.

As a small business owner thinking about marketing, your first goal should be to establish an online presence. Customers *need* to be able to find you online. Your second goal should be to take advantage of that presence. For example, you might want to be online for any number of reasons:

- Attracting new leads or customers
- Broadening your market reach
- Selling directly to customers online
- Connecting with customers to provide better service
- Distributing information about your products
- Establishing authority within your industry

To meet your goals, you need to create a distinctive and useful website *without* turning your business into a Web-design company. You need a website, but you can't afford to get sucked into spending all your time building or running it.

You can see the detritus of failed attempts at small business sites all over the Web. They tend to share a number of characteristics:

- They're old.
- They're ugly.
- They contain outdated information, such as phone numbers and addresses.
- They're hard to find (Google ranks them low in search results).

That last attribute—poor search ranking—might actually be a dubious sort of blessing for these sites: at least those companies are spared the embarrassment of people actually *finding* all that outdated information!

You might know fellow business owners who have commissioned sites like these. Maybe one of them is yours. The stories behind them tend to involve major expenditures and difficult times spent wrangling Web developers. You know the ones: they speak only a strange dialect of technical gibberish and wouldn't recognize a deadline if they tripped over it.

But take heart! As small business websites have proliferated, so have methods for building them. There has been a quiet revolution in website design and hosting that brings professional, attractive, feature-rich sites within your reach without exposing you to all the hassles of yore. You can now find software and hosting packages that

- Offer low and predictable costs, or even fixed monthly rates

- Require minimal time investment to build and maintain sites

- Come with attractive designs so you don't have to hire professional designers

- Let you start small and expand on demand

- Include search optimization to help boost your Google ranking

- Are easy enough to administer that even nontechnical staff can manage them

For small businesses searching for these features, WordPress is the most popular tool on the Internet today. Will your business be the next to take advantage of its power and simplicity?

A RANGE OF POSSIBILITIES

When most people hear the word "WordPress," they think of blogs. But blogging is just one small subset of what your small business can do with WordPress.

WordPress is a flexible, extendable Content Management System (CMS). Content Management Systems do pretty much what it sounds like they do: help you manage content. And on the Internet, as Bill Gates forecasted way back in 1996, content is king.

WordPress wasn't the first CMS, and it is not the only one available today, but it has become far and away the most popular. And that's not *just* because it's free.

WordPress has a roughly 60% share of the online CMS market because it hits that sweet spot between power and usability. It's easy to set up, but it can scale to handle almost any Web-based task imaginable. It's an ideal solution for small businesses that need a website but don't have a lot of time or money to devote to building one. Here are some of WordPress's other benefits:

- You can activate or install it with one click in 20 minutes or less.

- You can add and change content easily using its friendly, intuitive user interface.

- You don't have to be a graphics wizard to make your site look good.

Creating a custom website for your business used to take professional designers and programmers months and cost an arm and a leg. Once it was done, changes were usually equally painful. Now, you can perform the same task with just a low, flat-rate subscription payment and your mouse-clicking finger.

Just because a WordPress site is easy to set up doesn't mean it lacks features. (Because of its extremely flexible and customizable plugin system, WordPress lets you extend your site in unique and powerful ways.)

Because of this flexibility, WordPress is used for everything from powering busy media websites like Vogue.com to providing a platform for full-fledged e-commerce storefronts like Boardshorts.com. Chuck Yeager's personal website runs on WordPress. So does Snoop Dogg's.

FIGURE 2 Chuck Yeager's website

FIGURE 3 Snoop Dogg's website

If you can imagine a business use for a website, chances are someone has used WordPress to do it. Some of the resulting websites, like Mashable.com, are direct descendants of blog-type sites. But your site doesn't have to be.

Other businesses have found success using WordPress for tasks almost entirely unrelated to blogging. For example, Boardshorts.com built a complete e-commerce, inventory, and customer-management system into the platform. Founded in 2012 by two Santa Cruz surfers, this niche retailer realized right away that social media integration and word of mouth would be important. They also wanted to provide more detailed information in more visual formats (such as videos and infographics) than their competitors. The WordPress platform allowed them to incorporate all of those things into their site *without* diving into the complexities of programming or graphic design.

But WordPress sites don't have to be customer-facing to be useful for businesses. WordPress sites get used for internal communications, knowledge bases, and training. Some of the WordPress plugins used to create online courses are so powerful that even institutions like the University of British Columbia are using them for e-learning websites. Using that platform, subject-matter experts who don't have a clue about Web programming can design and deliver interactive online training classes in days.

WordPress sites don't even have to be interactive to be useful. The variety of professionally designed graphics themes that are available and the ease of installing them make WordPress an easy option for businesses who want only basic online presence without spending a lot of time designing or maintaining their websites. These so-called "brochure" or "business card" websites are fast to create. They put a professional face on any organization, or even a whole country: the official website of Sweden runs on WordPress.

FIGURE 4 www.boardshorts.com

FIGURE 5 The official website of Sweden

The system is so easy to set up and publish that even individual products are increasingly getting their own dedicated niche-marketing pages. For example, author Tim Ferriss built a WordPress website exclusively to promote his book *The 4-Hour Chef*.

Here are some other popular uses for WordPress:

- Delivering webinars
- Hosting internal company intranets
- Hosting photo or media albums
- Powering invoicing systems
- Providing online help desks
- Coordinating projects
- Managing customer relationships

The real beauty of WordPress is that you don't have to pick just *one* of these uses. A built-in feature called Multisite allows any WordPress installation to run an unlimited number of sites off the same server. So your marketing site can exist side by side with your customer-service site, and both of them can coexist with your internal knowledge base.

With all that WordPress *can* do, the biggest challenge might be narrowing down what you *want* it to do.

MASHABLE

Mashable.com is a news and information website "for the Connected Generation" that, in 2005, was started as a fairly conventional WordPress blog by 19-year-old Pete Cashmore in Scotland.

Mashable was a one-man show, but Cashmore quickly built a community out of his readership by using the commenting and social-media tools available with the platform. The site was a side project that Cashmore started partially because it was something he could do in bed. But his insightful commentary and innovative use of Web-based media quickly caught on and exploded in popularity.

Today, Mashable has about 60 employees and offices in New York and San Francisco. In 2012, Cashmore made *Time* magazine's World's 100 Most Influential People list.

The Mashable website's layout is a far cry from the plain, linear blog format it initially used. It serves more than 40 million unique visitors per month and is estimated to generate monthly revenues of more than half a million dollars. But under the hood, it's still based on the same WordPress software that it started out with.

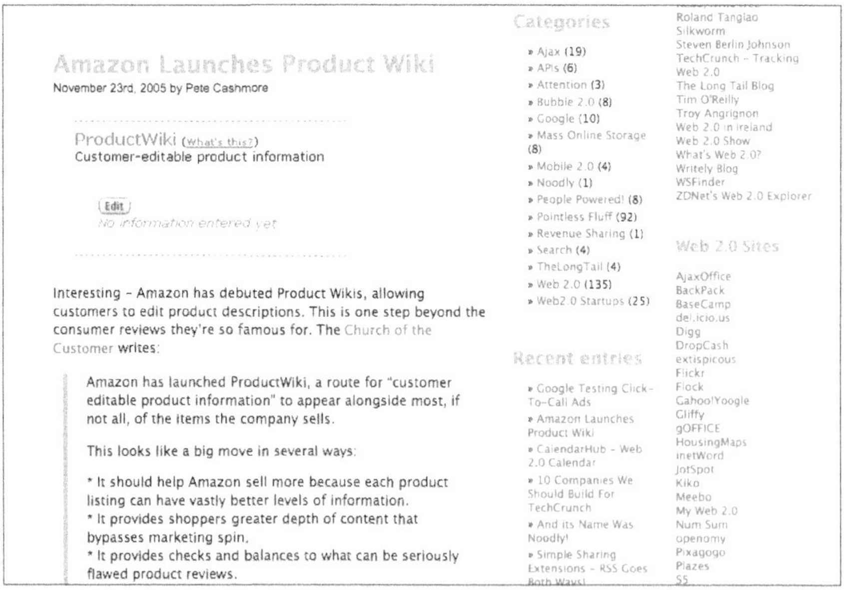

FIGURE 6 Mashable.com in November 2005

FIGURE 7 Mashable.com in June 2010

FIGURE 8 Mashable.com in May 2015

SETTING YOUR GOALS

If you're already running a business, then you know how important it is to set goals and stick to them. The same is true for your company's website. In fact, the goals you want to accomplish with your website are directly related to the goals you want to achieve with your business overall. (Your website exists to support and enable your business goals.) It can do so in one of five ways:

1. *Marketing:* This type of site can help you with branding, lead genera- tion, or just basic credibility.

2. *Interaction:* These sites can improve your community building and customer service or help you coordinate business or activities.

3. *E-commerce:* E-commerce sites allow you to sell products directly to customers.

4. *Media:* A media website is designed to tell your story or display information.

5. *Hybrid:* The great thing about WordPress is that you're not restricted to just one type of site or another; your website can combine elements from some or all of these categories!

Think about what you hope to accomplish with your company's website and the resources you can put into it. That will help you choose which type of site to create. Consider these factors as you're setting your goals:

- What value will your website offer? Since content is king, you need to think about what kind of content you can provide. No amount of bells, whistles, or cool designs will make up for content that no one cares about.

- Carefully define your target audience. Can you even reach them on the Internet? What types of devices will they use to access your site? What will they be looking for? Resist the temptation to define customers broadly; the more specific you can be, the more likely they will find you.

- Think about the ongoing demands your website might create. A media site, for example, will quickly grow stale and uninteresting without regu- lar, quality content updates. A marketing (a.k.a. brochure) site, however, might work perfectly well once set up and forgotten.

It's a good idea to do some research to get an idea of the possibilities for websites. Become familiar with what your competitors are doing online. This is the perfect excuse to sit around in front of your computer and surf the Internet. It's not slacking off, it's research!

If you aren't sure where to find examples, the official WordPress showcase site is a great place to go for ideas: https://wordpress.org/showcase.

Once you have some idea of what sort of site will best support your business goals, it's time to get specific. Your goals should all fit into the SMART format; they should be:

Specific: The goal should be well-defined. For example, "have a kick-ass comment form" isn't good enough. Be detailed and clear about what makes that comment form kick ass.

Measurable: You need to establish metrics that can objectively indicate whether the site is achieving the specific objective you set.

Actionable: The goal needs to be something you can exert control over. If you set a specific and measurable goal but can't think of a plan of action that lets you achieve it, it's not a smart goal.

Realistic: The goal shouldn't exceed the realm of possibility. Everyone loves stories like the twelve-year-old kid who launched a website out of his parent's basement and made $2 million dollars in six months, but those cases are the exceptions. Most websites fight hard for traffic and never get as much as their creators hope.

Time bound: Put specific time frames around your objectives. Be realistic about how long it will take to accomplish them. At the same time, don't make them open-ended. If you don't have a time limit, you may not know when to start making adjustments.

WHAT ARE YOUR GOALS?

Maybe you haven't yet thought a lot about what you can do with your website. That's okay—this is the perfect time to sit down and figure it out. Use this questionnaire to help brainstorm some goals for your website.

WHAT IS YOUR MOST IMPORTANT GOAL FOR THE WEBSITE?
For example, is it to increase sales, educate customers, or build your public profile? Write down the thing you most want to have achieved in six months.

WHAT ARE YOUR SECONDARY GOALS? If you accomplished the big one, are there any other outcomes you envision achieving with the site? List them here.

WHAT VALUE WILL THE WEBSITE OFFER TO PEOPLE WHO FIND IT?
(If you can't answer this question, you shouldn't be building a site!)

WHO IS YOUR TARGET AUDIENCE?

ONCE THE SITE HAS BEEN CREATED, WHAT ONGOING DEMANDS WILL IT PUT ON YOUR BUSINESS? For instance, will you have to keep creating content for it? Will it result in customer contacts to be followed up on? Are sales going to be generated that you will have to fulfill?

NOW, IT'S TIME TO GET SMART. Let's take a closer look at your most important goal, in light of the other information you listed. Write down how your main goal is:

Specific:

Measurable:

Attainable:

Realistic:

Time bound:

WHAT KIND OF WORDPRESS USER ARE YOU?

You know you want to build a website for your business, but what if you're not quite sure what sort of website you need? This quick quiz will help guide your thoughts on the ideal site for you.

1. WHAT IS THE VALUE THAT YOU WANT YOUR WEBSITE TO OFFER USERS?

A. They'll be able to buy goods or services directly from us.
B. They'll be able to receive help or support for our products.
C. They'll learn information about topics of interest.
D. They'll learn about our business and achievements.

2. WHAT AUDIENCE DO YOU HOPE TO REACH WITH YOUR WEBSITE?

A. New customers
B. Current customers, to improve sales and provide more information
C. People with a general interest in our industry
D. Prospective customers investigating our products or services

3. HOW FREQUENTLY WILL YOU BE ABLE TO UPDATE YOUR WEBSITE?

A. Only when new products come out.
B. Not very often—only when we have something to share.
C. Frequently. We want to keep people updated.
D. Rarely. We want to create our content and let people find it.

4. HOW MUCH FEEDBACK DO YOU HOPE TO GET FROM CUSTOMERS ON YOUR SITE?

A. Only when it comes in the form of a new order!
B. A lot! We want to hear everything people have to tell us.
C. A little. Most of the information should flow from us to them.
D. None. We just want to tell our story and allow people to read it.

5. HOW DOES YOUR TARGET AUDIENCE USE THE INTERNET?

A. They never even leave the house! If it weren't for Amazon Fresh, they'd starve to death.
B. They're on Facebook all day, chatting with their friends.
C. They surf and lurk a lot but don't interact much with others online.
D. They aren't online very often; they only use the Internet for specific research.

RESULTS

MOSTLY A: You are probably going to want an e-commerce website. You'll be most interested in the "Get Paid" chapter!

MOSTLY B: You need a primarily interactive website. Pay most attention to the "Interact" chapter.

MOSTLY C: You may be building a media website. Look closely at the "Create Content" and "Feature It" chapters.

MOSTLY D: You need a marketing (or "brochure") website. Pay attention to the "Create Content" and "Be Easy to Find" chapters.

PART

2

YOUR
WORDPRESS SITE

One reason for WordPress's popularity is that it makes many aspects of building a website as simple as choosing items from an à la carte menu. You might not have a website now, but after making the choices in this section you will have a unique, dynamic website for your business . . . and you can even start selling your product on it.

BUILD A HOME

Building a website is like building a house. You're going to think about the layout, color scheme, and amenities. You'll consider accessibility and ongoing maintenance. And at some point, you'll probably even have to delve into the plumbing a little bit. So you should approach the website-creation process with a similar mind set:

- Is the website you're building going to be a comfortable home for your business? Are visitors going to want to hang out there? Can you hold their interest?

- Will it be easy for visitors to find what they're looking for?

- How much is construction going to cost? Will you need to bring in specialists, or will you embrace a do-it-yourself approach?

- What will your long-term maintenance expenses be? Will the site hold up over the years, or do you anticipate changes and updates over time?

Many of these considerations are going to be addressed by the theme you choose. A WordPress theme is a collection of files that define the layout and style of your website. This includes things like fonts, colors, and columns and how headers, footers, and sidebars are laid out. Different themes allow differing degrees of customization without digging into the underlying code.

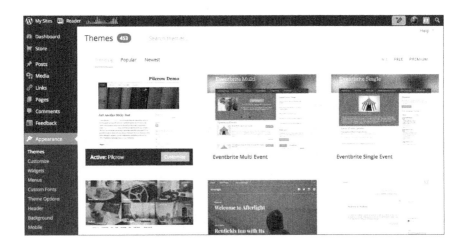

FIGURE 9

Every WordPress installation uses a theme. The software comes with a default theme called Twenty Fifteen. (Last year, the theme was named Twenty Fourteen. Want to guess what it will be next year?) But one of the first things WordPress does when you log in is encourage you to change your theme!

Picking a theme other than the default is a good idea. Not only do you not want to look like every other site that just installed WordPress, but it's also important to wrap your head around just how easy changing the theme can be.

CHOOSING A HOST

But we're getting ahead of ourselves! Before you can start building, you have to provide a foundation for your new website home. In technical terms, that means you need to find a host.

A host is a powerful computer, called a server, that can power all the under-the-hood code and data that serve a website to its users. Technically minded folks can simply rent a generic server from a provider at a data center or even build their own and install WordPress directly. But for the less technically inclined, finding a hosting provider who offers WordPress is the better option.

If you've roamed around the Internet looking at WordPress stuff, you might have noticed something odd: there are *two* main WordPress sites, WordPress.org and WordPress.com.

WordPress.org is the primary distribution and support hub for the WordPress software. WordPress is developed primarily under the auspices of the nonprofit WordPress Foundation. The foundation merely coordinates the development; much of the code is contributed by volunteers and third-party developers from the vast support ecosystem that has evolved around WordPress. The code is *open-source,* which means that anyone can look at and rewrite or extend it.

A condition of the WordPress license (called the "General Public License") requires that any such extensions or improvements must likewise be made freely available. That's why WordPress is free to download and install, assuming you have a server to install it on.

WordPress.com, however, is a hosting provider run by a different company entirely, Automattic. Automattic provides WordPress *hosting,* which means they maintain the servers that the software runs on. And boy, do they do a lot of hosting. WordPress.com handles 126 million unique visitors per month, spread across all their hosted sites. That's 30 million more than Amazon.com (one of the heavyweights of the Internet universe) sees each month.

There are pluses and minuses to using WordPress.com.

Advantages

- The basic service is free! You have to pay a fee to register your own domain name (you're not *required* to have your own domain name, but as a business, anything less will look unprofessional) but basic hosting with three gigabytes of storage will cost you nothing.
- No setup process is required.
- You'll get your site online instantly.
- All updates, maintenance, backups, and other nitty-gritty aspects of server administration are taken care of.

Drawbacks

- WordPress.com reserves the right to run ads on your website. You can't pick the ads, and you don't get any of the revenue they earn.
- Many of the options that make WordPress powerful are restricted:

  You can't install your own plugins.

  The themes you're allowed to use are restricted.

  You're not allowed to run your own advertising or sell anything directly by e-commerce.

  The Multisite option, which allows you to create any number of websites with a single administrative backend, is not available.
- You're at the mercy of the WordPress.com terms of service and their own business imperatives. Their priority is their own bottom line. They aren't working for you; they're working for their advertisers and subscribers. You have little recourse if your site is suspended for any reason.

Of course, you can pay to remove many of these limitations. Depending on your goals, this might be a worthwhile option to explore. However, you'll find that to get anywhere close to the full power of the WordPress platform, you'll have to pony up thousands of dollars a month—probably not the cheapest option.

If you download the software from WordPress.*org* instead, you instantly have the full power of the platform at your fingertips. Install any plugin, use any theme! The Web is your oyster.

But you will have other obstacles to wade through. For starters, you need a foundation to build your site on. So how do you get one?

You will have to buy or rent your own server and set it up or pay someone else to set it up for you. You'll also have the ongoing time or expense of maintaining it. And if your Internet provider charges for bandwidth use, you'll be dealing with that expense as well.

With great power comes great responsibility! Namely, you're going to be the one responsible for cleaning out your site's "plumbing" if the pipes get clogged.

Fortunately, your choice is not as stark as the .com and .org options presented above might make it appear. WordPress.com isn't the only company that offers WordPress hosting. WordPress is behind almost 25% of all websites, and it didn't get that way by being available in only two places!

Many other Web-hosting providers (including all the most popular ones) offer automated or semiautomated WordPress installation and hosting for a nominal fee. One-click installation is the norm.

Better yet, those providers offer a spectrum of services that take many of the menial tasks of server maintenance off your hands while still allowing you to make full use of WordPress's power and flexibility. In the Resources section (page 108) at the end of this book, you'll find links to websites that list recommended hosting providers. Alternatively, WordPress.org has a Hosting section that lists recommended hosting providers.

PICKING A THEME

Once your foundation is laid, it's time to start putting up the walls by choosing the website's theme.

Your goals will probably help you decide on a theme. Themes are as varied as the developers who produce them. Some are complicated and difficult to work with; others are straightforward and a pleasure to build with. Then there's the issue of attractiveness. Put plainly, some themes are well done and others aren't.

You'll spend a lot of time looking at and thinking about themes. There are more than 10,000 WordPress themes available today, with more being created all the time. Some are free, and some cost more than $100. All of them have certain things in common:

- Many of the nuts and bolts of website construction are already taken care of for you.

- The basics of usability, standards, and browser compatibility are addressed by the theme.

- The theme offers a set of templates, which allows you to concentrate on your content without having to think about harmonizing how it's displayed.

- The theme determines how many columns, post formats, and (sometimes) colors will be used. In a good theme, those will all be coordinated for a consistent look and feel.

You're not limited to just what you can find in the theme catalogs. If for some reason none of the themes listed there tickles your fancy, you can always pay a theme developer to create your own special version.

Many themes are designed specifically for certain types of websites. For example, some themes are intended for e-commerce sites. Others are configured for media sites, and others for marketing and brand awareness. Most theme providers clearly indicate what their themes are designed for, and they're not shy about advertising the best features.

Beyond the cost, appearance, and options, there are a number of other factors to consider when choosing a theme:

FIGURE 10

Support: Free themes don't usually offer support. If you have a problem, you're on your own. But even premium theme providers vary in how often they release updates and fix bugs.

Speed: A fast website is key to good user experience. Themes with a lot of bells and whistles may look impressive, but all those options may make them as slow as molasses.

Search optimization: Your theme has a lot to do with how easily Google and other search engines can survey your site, and thus how they will rank you in their results. Some themes use search engine optimization (SEO) to boost those rankings.

Browser compatibility: Themes use various tricks of display and layout, which aren't always interpreted the same way by different Web browsers. If the theme's developer tested it with Firefox but not Internet Explorer and most of your audience is likely to use Internet Explorer, you might have a problem.

Theme selection is consequential, but it's not permanent. If you happen to pick the wrong theme to start with, it's not the end of the world. WordPress is wonderfully adaptable, and you can select almost any options during theme setup without fear of being locked into them forever. So don't let picking the perfect theme paralyze you.

Once you've selected a theme, installing it is easy. In fact, if you're install-ing a free theme from the official WordPress theme directory, it's *super* easy. You can do it right from your Dashboard administration screen:

1. In the left-hand column, click Appearance.

2. On the Themes menu screen, click Add New. You'll be presented with the same catalog you found on WordPress.org.

3. Hover your cursor over the theme you want, and then click Install. The theme will automatically be downloaded and installed.

4. If you want to make the newly downloaded theme active, just click Activate at the bottom of the screen. Or you can preview it first.

Installing a premium theme or free theme from another source usually only requires one additional step. You'll have downloaded the theme file (a ZIP format file) and then, instead of clicking Add New in step 2, you'll click Upload Theme and choose the theme file on your computer to upload it to your site.

Sometimes, particularly feature-heavy themes will require additional steps. In those cases, the theme's creator will supply step-by-step installa-tion instructions.

Once the theme is installed and activated, you can start playing with its various options. In the left-hand column of your Dashboard administra-tion screen, point to the word "Appearance," and then choose Customize. Different themes will offer different options here. They typically include colors, column layout, and menu structure. You might have to consult the theme's documentation for descriptions of some of the options.

Some themes—particularly free ones—offer no Customize options at all. Other themes have more options than can squeeze into the Customize menu. In those cases, you'll usually find more options under the Appearance menu that allow you to customize the theme. Again, theme-specific documentation should provide more details on what your options are and how to use them.

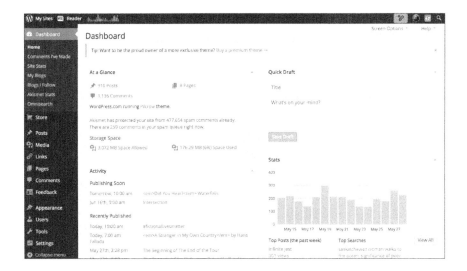

FIGURE 11

FIGURE 12

LAY IT OUT

You've selected a hosting provider, got your domain name, and set up your WordPress website. You thought about your business goals and figured out what you want your site to accomplish. You've picked out a theme that will support those goals, downloaded it, and activated it. You probably spent some time kicking the tires, changing the colors, and playing with menus. You must be exhausted! Take a minute to rest on your laurels. Maybe have a drink.

Because now it's time to log in and get to work.

Someone else built that theme for you, put effort into choosing colors and creating layouts, and made sure it worked in a bunch of different browsers. They made it easy for you to install, configure the theme, and probably even modify it a bit to make it your own.

But now you're coming to the hard part: You have to map out the site by deciding how to provide the functions and content you need to deliver to meet your business goals.

MODERN WEBSITE ARCHITECTURE

Most websites consist of multiple pages. The home page, or front page, is the first one that users will see when they type your site's address into their browsers. Clearly, that is a pretty important page—it creates people's first impression, and statistics show that users decide whether to stay or leave in only fractions of a second. So your site has to make the right first impression or you'll lose visitors.

Other pages are also important. (The pages you decide to create will depend on the type of site you want to have.) Here are some common pages that your website might have:

News: This is where you can post press releases and other exciting information you want to share with the press or customers.

Contact Us: This page tells people how to find your business. It can include things like phone numbers and e-mail addresses or a contact form, as well as a map, mailing address, and driving directions.

Thank You: Post customer appreciation notes and stories about your products here.

About Us: This is where you share the history of your company and a little about the owners and employees.

Privacy/Terms of Use: Boring (but important!) legalese belongs here.

Blog: This page is where you display a running series of posts talking about your products, your industry, or general information that's of interest to your customers.

Some of these pages may be more important to your goals than others. And some websites, such as e-commerce sites, will have many more types of pages, such as product specifications, support, documentation, and forums.

One way to help you visualize your website pages is to physically lay it all out using paper or 3×5 index cards.

Some pages may have sub-pages. For instance, a Contact Us page might have a sub-page with a map or directions to your offices.

Particularly complex sites often have pages that are automatically generated by a plugin (you'll learn about plugins and widgets in the Add Features chapter). E-commerce sites, for example, usually have product information that's stored in a database, and the plugin will automatically create a separate page for each product, complete with pictures, a description, and ordering information. Similarly, for blog sites, you simply create a new blog entry, and the theme creates a new page for it. You just have to input the information and select the template.

Even pages you build yourself are easy to create in WordPress. Permanent pages on your site are called static pages. You create and manage them using the Pages menu of the Dashboard administration screen.

More traditional blog-entry pages are called posts and are, of course, created and managed via the Posts menu.

The way you create both posts and pages is essentially identical. In either the Posts or Pages menu, clicking Add New will take you to the same editing console. So what are the differences between posts and pages?

Posts

- Are listed in reverse chronological order
- By default, are featured on the home page of the site
- Can be put into categories
- Can be labeled with tags
- Are great for providing regular and timely updates
- Appear in traditional blog format

Pages

- May be organized arbitrarily
- Can be nested
- Can be displayed in a structure of your choosing
- Are intended as a permanent feature of the site
- Contain text that is usually fixed
- Provide information that is neither timely nor likely to change frequently
- Can be included in menus

Whether you are working on a post or a page, the editor is where you'll be spending most of your time while you're building out your site, so you'd better get comfortable with it. The next section helps you do that.

FILLING IN THE BLANKS

Go ahead and click the word "Pages" on the left side of the Dashboard administration screen, and then click Add New.

This is the editor. Let's give it a spin, shall we?

1. The box at the top, just beneath the Add New Page heading, is for the title. Enter some text here.

2. The visual editor (the big box below the title) allows WYSIWYG ("what you see is what you get") entry of your content. Type in some text!

FIGURE 13

3. If you like, format your content. The visual editor works like a mini word processor. Most of the buttons above it should look familiar to anyone who has used Microsoft Word or any similar program. If you aren't sure what a button does, just hover your cursor over it and a description will appear after a few seconds. Just for kicks, highlight some of the text you just entered, then click the *I* to italicize it.

4. At the top right of the visual editor is a tab labeled "Text," which, somewhat confusingly, shows you the formatting codes and not just the text. This tab is typically used by more advanced users. Click it, and you should see <em> formatting marks around the text you italicized.

5. Okay, enough fun with that for now—click the Visual tab (it's right next to the Text tab) to get back to the main editor.

6. Above the toolbar you should see a button labeled "Add Media." This can be used to insert pictures, audio, or video into your pages. If you want to add a picture, go ahead and do that now. Depending on the plugins that you install, you may see more or fewer formatting and media options. For example, specialized plugins can offer more text formatting or media-embedding options.

7. What you've entered will be automatically saved in Draft form as you work (only editors like you can see drafts). If you want to save it manually, in the Publish box to the right of the title, click Save Draft. Go ahead and do that now.

8. Now, click Preview (it's next to the Save Draft button). A new window will open in your browser and show you what your content will look like in your current theme.

9. Close that new window. At this point, if you were ready to share your new page with the world, you could click Publish in the Publish box to make the page viewable to anyone. But for now, since you were just messing around, click "Move to Trash" instead, which gets rid of the whole thing.

So far, everything you've looked at on the editor will be identical for either a page or a post. Also, both pages and posts can be created as *drafts*, which are only visible to site editors, allowing you to work on them out of the public eye until you are satisfied with the results. But when you go beyond the title and visual editor boxes, differences begin to appear.

These disparities relate to the different natures of the two types of content. Pages, as mentioned earlier, can have a hierarchy, which means you have the option of setting a *parent* and *order* to determine how they will display relative to each other. Posts, however, have categories and tags that allow you to group them arbitrarily.

Depending on your theme, you may be able to select different templates for your pages that will optimize them for their intended purpose. For instance, you may not want sidebars or comments to show up on your Contact Us page, because they would distract users from the contact form or instructions. You can select a template that excludes those features by clicking on the Templates drop-down in the Page Attributes box on the right-hand side of the page and browsing the available templates. Just click Preview to see what your page will look like with different templates selected.

There is one special template that combines posts and pages: if you set a page's template to Blog, it will display posts *on that page*. This is ideal for a News page, for instance.

Featured images can be set for both posts and pages. Different themes may use these graphics in different ways; typically, a featured image is displayed at the top of the page or post. You can pick and add these through the Media Library like any other picture on your site.

Don't go overboard creating either posts or pages at first. You can always add them to your site later on. You still see websites that have "Coming Soon!" pages all over them. That just looks bad, and it looks worse the longer they sit there without anything substantive on them. Even worse are sites that contain content that was rushed out the door. Putting up something bad is worse than putting up nothing at all.

ADD FEATURES

WordPress is a very capable piece of software right out of the virtual box it came in, so it might surprise you to learn that it's actually designed to be relatively basic and lightweight. This means that it avoids cluttering up and slowing down websites that don't need a lot of extras.

A very basic marketing or brochure website doesn't need a lot of bells and whistles. Businesses with more ambitious goals, however, will find their time spent mostly in WordPress's powerful and adaptive plugin and widget system. Much of how your business will actually accomplish its goals will revolve around the plugins and widgets you pick and how you use them.

Plugins

- Were developed both by WordPress and third-party developers
- Can be custom made
- May alter both the appearance and function of the website
- May affect website performance
- Are easy to install, activate, or delete

Widgets

- Add content or features to sidebars
- Are simple and usually have a single purpose
- May come with plugins
- Do not alter the basic function of the website
- Cannot easily be added or removed independently of a theme or plugin

PLAYING WITH PLUGINS

Plugins can be added or managed through the Plugins administration screen.

Just as with themes, many plugins are free and can be viewed and added directly from the main WordPress.org repository by clicking Add New on the Plugins menu. Installation is just as easy: click Install Now and you're off (or follow the upload process for commercial plugins downloaded separately; it's the same as described previously for themes).

There are more than 36,000 WordPress plugins available today, so it's impossible to go into any sort of detail about the functions and settings of each one. Most include documentation about setup and configuration. Just to give you an example, however, we'll go through the process of setting up one plugin you already have: Akismet.

You already have it because it's one of only two plugins included with every default installation of WordPress. (The other is Hello Dolly, which randomly displays lyrics from the Louis Armstrong tune of the same name on your administration pages. Unless you're a huge Louis Armstrong fan, you'll probably find Akismet more useful.)

Akismet blocks comment spam *really well*. Around 7.5 million annoying Viagra-related comments per hour never pollute the Internet because Akismet catches them first. If you allow comments or feedback on your site, you'll quickly grow thankful for it. Untended spam is a huge red flag on a business website—it demonstrates a lack of attention that immediately discredits your business in the eyes of users.

Akismet is also a good example plugin because it works with a Web service, which means that part of it runs on your site, but most of the processing happens elsewhere. This is part of that whole "cloud" thing that you've probably heard about, and services of this sort are the future of the Internet. Increasingly, websites like yours are going to be interlinked and powered in part by Web services. So configuring Akismet is a good way to get used to the concept. Here's what you do:

1. If you're not already on the Plugins administration screen, click Plugins on the left side of your screen to display it.

2. You'll see Akismet near the top of the list of installed plugins. If you haven't changed anything, you'll see Activate, Edit, and Delete buttons beneath it. Click Activate.

FIGURE 14

3. Those buttons will change to Settings, Deactivate, and Delete. Click Settings.

4. Because it operates as a Web service, you'll need something called a key to proceed. There's a button that says "Get your API Key"; go ahead and click it.

5. You'll be taken to Akismet's website and asked to sign up for a WordPress .com account (if you don't have one already). Don't let this confuse you: even if you're not using WordPress.com to host your site, Akismet is run by the same company, so go ahead and sign up. Since you are building a website for commercial use, you will (eventually) need a paid account. If you don't want to deal with that now, don't worry about it. Just create a free personal account and you can change your plan later.

6. Once you're signed up, you'll be shown a random string of letters and numbers; this is your API key. Write it down!

7. Back on your website, the Akismet plugin should still be patiently waiting for that key. Type it into the box and then click "Use this key."

That's it! Akismet is now active, and any comment anyone posts on your site will swiftly and silently be screened. You can change some minor settings here; suspected spam comments will either be discarded automatically or simply set aside in a spam folder for your review. Also, a new item has appeared in your Settings menu: Akismet. Clicking it gives you access to these same settings in case you need to change them. It will also show you statistics on blocked spam.

Like Akismet, many plugins will add an entry to your Settings menu. Depending on their function, their settings options may be just as minimal as those for Akismet or bewilderingly complex.

One of the great things about the plugin system is the almost complete lack of commitment. You can install, activate, and deactivate plugins so effortlessly that it's almost *too* easy. Now that we've gone to all the trouble of getting Akismet set up, let's turn it off again, shall we?

You can access plugin settings from the Plugins menu, where you first installed Akismet. Go ahead and go back there by clicking Plugins again.

1. Find Akismet in the list, and click Deactivate beneath it.

2. Now click the Settings menu again. No Akismet! The plugin is installed but not operating. Spam will now run wild on your website.

3. Go back to Plugins, and activate Akismet again. (No one likes spam.)

It's so easy to download, install, and try out plugins that you can easily end up with way too many of them. They each take up storage space and, if activated, may drag down your site's performance. So it's a good idea to delete plugins that you've tried and found useless.

WORKING WITH WIDGETS

Widgets, however, are smaller and less consequential than plugins, and you cannot get rid of them. Let's play around with one to get a feel for the system.

1. On the left side of your screen, point your cursor at the word "Appearance" and then click Widgets. You'll see the widgets that are currently available, as well as a list of the sidebars (including headers and footers) available in your current theme. As you can see from the selection available, widgets tend to be small, single-function tools or tweaks (a calendar or a list of recent comments, for example).

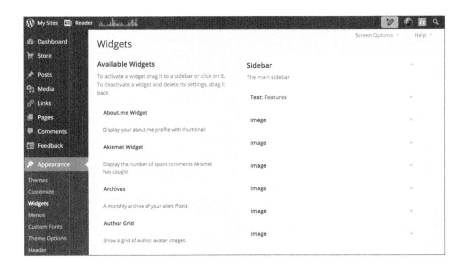

FIGURE 15

2. You can either drag and drop widgets from the left-hand column onto sidebars in the right-hand column or click the widget you want to add in the left-hand column, then select the desired sidebar from the list that appears, and click Add Widget. For now, find the Search widget on the left and drag it onto one of the sidebars.

3. Now, under your site's name in the upper-left corner of the window, click View Site. A search bar should now appear on the sidebar where you added it.

4. Go back to your Dashboard, and then, on the left side of the screen, point to the word "Appearance," and click Widgets. You can remove the widget as easily as you added it—just drag it out of the sidebar and back over to Available Widgets, and it will disappear from the sidebar.

Widgets, like plugins, can have settings. These are separate for each sidebar in which the widget appears. The most common setting is the title. For example, if you want Search to be displayed as Find Stuff instead, you can change that in the Title setting on a particular sidebar. Other widgets will have other display options; just click the widget in the sidebar to see what they are.

MANAGING MEDIA FILES

Something else that should feature prominently on your business site is images. There are a number of reasons for this:

- The Internet is a visual medium.

- Images increase the appeal of your site; websites that don't have images and videos are less appealing than those that do.

- Many search engines incorporate images into their search algorithms, so not having images can mean lower search rankings for your site.

WordPress has a built-in Media Library feature that helps you add, organize, and incorporate audio, video, and images without having to think too much about the complexities of file types and sizes. Using the Media Library is a good way for you to maintain standards for media to be displayed on your site. You want high-quality, clearly labeled media.

Make sure that you aren't violating any copyrights for any media you display—a quick way to get blacklisted on Google is to have a copyright holder complain that you do not have permission to display his or her work on your site.

You can view your library by clicking Media on the left side of your Dashboard administration screen. What do you have in the library so far— nothing, eh? Well, let's fix that.

1. Find an image somewhere on your computer. Click it and drag it onto the Media Library screen. If the picture is on your desktop, for example, just click and drag it on top of the grid and then release your mouse button. It will be uploaded and added automatically. Congratulations! You now have media in your media library. (You can also add videos or audio clips to the Media Library. Once you have several media files in your library, you can filter the Media Library to show only images, videos, or audio clips, or you can search by keywords if you've applied any.)

2. Click the new image. An Attachment Details screen will come up providing a closer look and some additional details. You can change the title and add a caption (shown beneath the picture), alt text (read or displayed to visually impaired users), and a description (shown in most themes when a user clicks the image). It's a good idea to fill in these fields, so you can use the search feature in the future to find images by keywords.

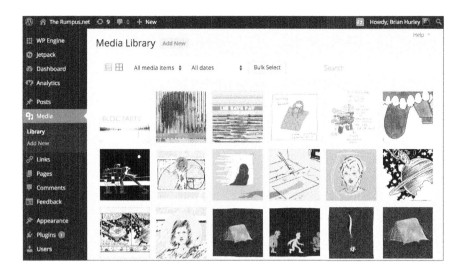

FIGURE 16

3. Fill in the Alt Text field with a short description of the image. In addition to helping visually impaired visitors to your site, this info is also used by search engines.

4. Click the Edit Image button below the image.

5. If you like, rotate, crop, flip, or alter the dimensions of the uploaded image if it's not quite right as is. When you're done editing, click Save.

6. Each item in your library also gets its own automatically generated page. Click "View attachment page" to see what this looks like in your theme.

Items from the Media Library can be easily added to any post or page when working in the visual editor; simply click Add Media. When you do that, you see all the items in your library. If you click one, you'll see the attachment details you specified (caption, alt text, etc.). Below that are settings that let you set the specific details of how the item will display in your text. Use the Alignment menu to set it to appear to the left, right, or center of the screen, and select a size. WordPress automatically creates several size options (you can control the default image sizing in the Settings menu under Media), so you don't have to worry about the original image size.

POPULAR WORDPRESS PLUGINS

AKISMET: The Big Kahuna of plugins, Akismet is so important it is one of only two plugins installed by default. Akismet does nothing without an alphanumeric key from the Akismet service (run by Automattic, the folks behind WordPress.com); with a key, it becomes a powerful spam-fighting demigod watching over your site. Subscriptions for commercial websites start at a reasonable $5 per month.

ALL IN ONE SEO PACK: This plugin tweaks your site behind the scenes to improve the ability of search engines to catalog and present it to searchers.

CONTACT FORM 7: A simple but powerful contact form that allows you to create e-mail contact forms for your site.

GOOGLE XML SITEMAPS: A sitemap is a digital diagram of how all the pages on your website tie together. You probably don't care all that much about this diagram, but Google puts a lot of faith in them, and having one is important for search engine optimization (SEO), which you'll learn more about in later chapters. This plugin creates a sitemap and otherwise stays out of your way.

JETPACK: Jetpack is a potpourri plugin that contains a little bit of everything to pep up your site. It promises to improve performance, security, and engagement, along with a host of other tweaks and features.

WOOCOMMERCE: This free e-commerce toolkit allows you to easily create product catalogs and sell products directly from your site.

Each of these plugins will have alternatives created by other programmers; someone is always trying to build a better mousetrap. You might find that you prefer one of the alternatives, so don't be afraid to check them out.

As with WordPress themes, some plugins cost money and others are free. Commercial plugins usually (but not always) offer better support and features.

If you're creating a post or page and discover that the item you want isn't in your Media Library, simply click the Upload Files tab and then add the file you want. Or, if you don't have the image file on your computer, you can click the "Insert from URL" option on the left. Pull up the image you want in your Web browser, and then paste in the URL address and click "Insert into page." WordPress will create a link to that picture and insert it into your text.

Of course, the Media Library can work only with what you give it. Some images may be too big or not big enough, and the options WordPress offers you may be limited. Still, the system will take a lot of the thinking out of creating and sizing images for your site and simplify the process of adding media. Say good-bye to your expensive graphic designer!

GET ORGANIZED

Many business owners have a bit of a blind spot when it comes to their own businesses: since they already know everything about their businesses, it's hard to imagine how best to tell potential customers and website visitors about it.

WordPress has a lot of options to help people find what they're looking for on your website. How you configure these things will determine how easy it is for users to connect with the information you want them to see.

MANAGING PAGE MENUS

You already determined a structure of sorts when you laid out your pages. Now, you'll need to put that structure into a menu so it will show up on your site. Your theme will likely include menu locations built into the templates. Most themes support multiple menus, including:

- Primary navigation: May also be called the "main" menu; is usually displayed prominently on each page template.
- Mobile menu: A special menu scheme shown only to users on mobile devices. You can simplify the structure to display only pages with mobile utility here.

- Top-bar navigation: If the primary navigation menu isn't in the top bar of the website, a top-bar menu may be available to provide another layer of navigation.

- Footer menu: These often include less-frequently referenced pages such as legal or contact information.

Menus can include any number of pages, and those pages can appear on different levels of the menu. The order of pages in a menu does not have to patch the order of pages on the site.

Here's how to create some menus for your site:

1. On the left side of your screen, put your cursor over the word "Appearance," and then click the Menus item that appears. You probably already have a menu here (called Main), but let's create a new one to play with.

2. Click "Create a new menu."

3. Type a name for the menu in the Menu Name box (you can just call this one "Secondary" if you like), then click Create Menu.

4. On the left, you'll see a list of your available pages (by default, the most recently created pages will be shown, but you can click the View All or Search tabs if you have a lot to sift through). Check the boxes for several of them, then click Add to Menu.

5. The selected pages will show up on the right. You can click and drag them around into your preferred order. If you want one page nested under another, drag it onto the top-level page and it will show up in a hierarchy.

6. Below the list of pages in the menu are the menu options:

   - You can check "Auto add pages" to make sure the menu is automatically updated when a new page is created; the new page will show up at the bottom of the menu.

   - You can also check boxes for the theme menu locations to automatically use this new menu for any of them.

7. When you're finished, click Save Menu.

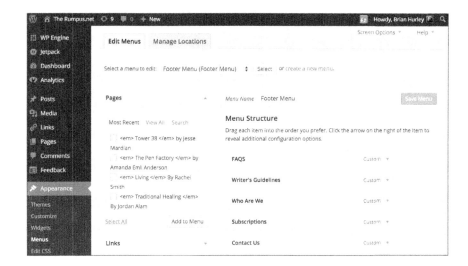

FIGURE 17

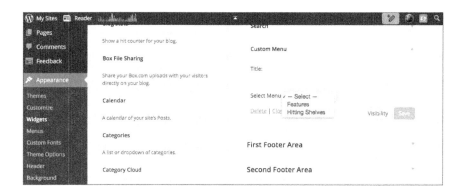

FIGURE 18

Once menus have been created, you manage them in much the same way as you added them. You do so using the same Menus screen, which you access via the Appearance menu on the left.

On the Menus screen, you can change which menus are displayed in which theme locations by clicking the Manage Locations tab. All the available locations will be shown with the option to switch which menu is used for each of them or to show no menu at all. You don't want to overwhelm your users, so make your navigation scheme both sensible and minimal!

If for some reason your theme doesn't include built-in menu locations, you're not out of luck. WordPress comes with a Custom Menu widget that can be included in any sidebar. You define your menu structure as described above, but instead of using the Manage Locations option, just go into the Widgets administration screen (it's also listed under the Appearance menu on the left side of your screen) and drag the Custom Menu widget onto the desired sidebar. Once it's in place, you can give it a label like any other widget. You will also see a drop-down box with an option to pick your defined menu.

TAGGING AND CATEGORIZING POSTS

Posts are organized differently than menus. By default, on any page where they are displayed, posts will show up in reverse chronological order with the most recent entry at the top of the page.

That system works just fine when you're presenting material to users who are keeping up with it regularly or when the information becomes irrelevant once some time has passed. It's a great way to keep your site looking fresh and up-to-date.

But there may be valuable information about your products, business, or industry that is buried in all those old posts. Tagging and categorizing the posts when they are created will keep all that valuable content easily accessible for your customers. Here's what each feature does:

Tags

- Are usually more numerous than categories, so use as many tags as you need
- Tend to be more specific than categories
- Are nonhierarchical

- Are free-form
- Are optional—you don't *need* to use them
- Can be converted into categories

Categories

- Can have a hierarchy
- Have a more rigid structure than tags
- Are usually scarcer than tags
- Are broader in scope than tags
- Are required; every post must belong to at least one category

Tags were invented to take some of the pressure off of categories. You can think of categories as the primary way to organize posts. If you were writing a book, categories would be the chapters: the way that you, the author, intend to organize the content for presentation to the reader.

Tags are like the index, a way for the reader to dive into specific topics that might be covered in multiple chapters for various reasons.

You can create categories and tags using the corresponding menu items under the Posts menu on the left side of the Dashboard administration screen. Alternatively, you can create them on the fly when you're adding or editing a post.

FIGURE 19

TAXONOMY TIPS

Sometimes, people go a little crazy with tags and categories. You don't want to end up with a classification system that's more confusing than the underlying information. Creating a taxonomy is one way to avoid ending up with a spaghetti mess of tags and categories.

A taxonomy is just a classification system. You probably already have something like this in your business, but the system you use on your website will probably be different: it needs to classify things in ways that will make sense to your customers. Here are some guidelines:

THINK ABOUT YOUR AUDIENCE. They will be coming in to your site with a certain mind set, looking for certain things. How can you best present your content to answer their likely questions?

THINK ABOUT THE INFORMATION YOU NEED TO CATEGORIZE. Are there natural ways to group it or a hierarchy it should fall into?

CONSIDER WHO WILL BE CREATING YOUR CONTENT. If you're doing it yourself, then you will probably create a consistent taxonomy without even thinking about it. But if employees or contractors will be building your content, you may need to set out a shared taxonomy before they get started.

KEEP IT AS SIMPLE AS POSSIBLE. Presenting users with a long list of words with trivial or incomprehensible differences is not any help. Make clear distinctions and use common words to label them!

AVOID DUPLICATES AND CHECK YOUR SPELLING! When you're creating labels on the fly, be aware that minor spelling differences will result in completely separate classifications.

The taxonomy is not about your business processes, but instead about your customers or users. The way you deliver products and services may differ dramatically from how they perceive it. So keep in mind that a taxonomy that's useful to your staff might not be helpful for your customers.

Inevitably, after you've been using tags and categories for a while, you'll find some duplication or misspelling in one of them. Fortunately, management and cleanup is easy.

- On their respective screens (which you select from the Posts menu), you can see and edit or delete all tags and categories that have been created.

- The screen will also show you a frequency count, so you can tell how often they've been used. You might get rid of infrequently used items to reduce clutter.

- You can enter a longer description, which is useful if other people edit your site—be clear about what the label is for.

- You can also edit the "slug" that is automatically generated. This version of the label is used in the URL and helps search engines find your site.

- You can convert tags into categories (though not vice versa) if you find a particular tag worthy of promotion. To do so, in the Tags administration screen, click the "Tag to category converter" link.

Like most of your choices in WordPress, you can change your mind with how you use tags and categories at almost any time and the software will let you do it. Your audience, however, won't appreciate you changing up your site once they've learned their way around. So invest some time in organizing early on and, once you go live, make changes only after due consideration.

BE EASY TO FIND

The breadth and depth of the Internet is overwhelming. It's easy to get lost in detail when you're surfing or searching, endlessly sidetracked by one fascinating bit of information after another.

As a small business trying to get your site noticed on the Web, this vastness is something you will be perpetually fighting. Just getting found is the number one obstacle for most businesses to overcome with their websites.

One thing that can help is a process called search engine optimization (SEO). As you were looking through themes and plugins for your site, you probably saw this term frequently.

FIGURE 20

An SEO-friendly theme is the best place to start this process. Fortunately, almost all themes are designed, in at least some sense, to be search-engine friendly. SEO will be a factor for you to consider when choosing a theme, but probably not the overwhelming one. Looks and functionality will be more important. That's because SEO in the WordPress world is heavily driven by plugins. You'll find a lot of debates over which is best, but for the average small business, almost any of plugin will cover the basics, so just pick one you're comfortable using.

Google, the granddaddy of all search engines, provides a simple starters' guide to help your site rank well in search results. Appropriately, this guide is the first result when you search Google for "search engine optimization" (you can also find a link to it in the Resources section of this book; see page 108), and everyone who operates a small business website should review it. The gist is that you need to make your content relevant and describe it accurately with titles and keywords.

A title is the title of a post or page. You enter it in the Title field in the Visual Editor and possibly use it in menus or SEO plugin settings. Keywords are a series of words or phrases that concisely describe the content of a post or page. You'll probably use some of these words as part of the title, in any descriptions you assign, or independently in a variety of SEO tools.

Here's what you need to know about these features:

MEET BARRY

Barry is 33 and balding. He smokes Kool milds and enjoys strawberry margaritas and taking long walks on the beach.

No, Barry didn't escape from the set of *Miami Vice* to emerge here via a time warp. Barry is a wholly fabricated model of your ideal customer; he's a *profile*.

Profiles are imaginary but detailed personifications of likely customers or website users you're trying to reach. You might create one or more profiles to represent each category of user for your site. Here are some tips for creating profiles:

- Use profiles to help escape from the constraints of your own deep knowledge of the business. They are a way to put yourself in the shoes of your users.

- Start with a broad perspective on your audience. Then see if you can pick out one or more types of user that you expect to attract.

- Once you have a general picture, start to flesh it out with more detail. Give your imaginary user a name, age, gender, and ethnicity. As you add more details, imagine how these motivate that person. Do your site colors remind Barry of those ocean sunsets he loves? Can he still navigate your categories after a few margaritas?

Build your list of profiles early on in your design process and refer back to the list frequently. Every decision you make should be reviewed in terms of how your profile audience will view it.

Titles

- Should be unique; don't use the same title for more than one page or post on your website.
- Feature the most important keywords first. If you're trying to impress people with your innovative lemon cinnamon roll recipe, don't title it "Lemons and innovation lead to terrific-tasting cinnamon rolls!" Instead, start with the most relevant words, like this: "Lemon cinnamon rolls are a terrific-tasting innovation!"
- Should contain your brand name in them somewhere.
- Need to be catchy enough to be clickable! You'll want to stand out on the results page as much as possible.
- Should not be longer than 70 characters. They may get cut off if they're longer than that.

Keywords

- Should accurately reflect the content of the post
- Should be included frequently in the post itself
- Should be considered in the comments and how comments might affect the frequency of keywords for a given post or page. If you intend to allow site users to comment on your posts, be aware that the words they use may affect the balance of word frequency for search engine indexes. This can be good or bad for you, but either way it will largely be outside your control.

Web pages can also have descriptions associated with them—text that doesn't appear on the page itself but is provided to search engines and Web browsers. Many SEO plugins allow you to enter these descriptions manually along with page titles and keywords.

- Descriptions should be a short sales pitch for clicking the post.
- Like titles, descriptions should be unique.

These are Google's guidelines, but they'll serve you well for ranking highly in almost *any* search engine.

Most SEO plugins will allow you to tweak these details, and many of them will prompt you if you go off the rails, letting you know if your title is too long or your keywords irrelevant. Some can provide a detailed analysis of your content from a search engine's perspective, suggesting ways to rewrite your text to improve it.

COURTING YOUR SEARCH ROBOT OVERLORDS

Plugins are also your best option to generate another Google-recommended site feature: a sitemap. A sitemap is just an outline of your site, rendered in a format that is easy for computers to read. In the same way that a good menu and category structure helps users find pages and posts on your site, a sitemap can help search-engine indexers (called "spiders" because they crawl the Web—get it?) find everything you want them to see.

Without a sitemap, spiders rely on advanced algorithms and link recursion. These are pretty good techniques, but you don't want to leave it up to chance—search results can't show anything that spiders can't index.

There's another factor to consider with sitemaps and spiders, which is that you might *not* want some of your site's content to appear in search results. For instance, you might have pages on your site that won't be helpful as a first step for your audience to land on. A checkout or thank-you page is oriented at folks who have just bought something from you. A searcher coming in from Google doesn't fit into that category and isn't likely to be impressed with what they see there, so you're wasting your time and theirs if you allow this type of page to be indexed.

Most Web crawlers respect the content of a file called robots.txt on your site, which tells them what you do and don't want indexed. WordPress includes this file by default, but it initially only blocks access to internal WordPress code files; it may not cover other items you want to exclude. Here, again, plugins will come to your rescue. Several are available that allow you to customize your robots.txt file.

If all this is starting to sound overwhelming and you're uncertain of how you're doing, Google can (again) offer some assistance. Google Webmaster Tools (https://www.google.com/webmasters/tools) can give you a glimpse of how Google sees your site and tell you about common errors it might have encountered there.

Perhaps surprisingly, one of the things that Google emphasizes is to *not* think too much about optimizing your site for their index. Their goal is to show their users the best results to satisfy the search query. A website written for a robot spider probably won't do that. So their suggestion is that you focus on making content useful to your audience.

Doing this serves you in two ways: first, you won't waste time trying to second-guess indexing algorithms; second, however users ultimately end up on your site, they'll be more likely to find it useful.

On or off the Internet, word of mouth is valuable. And the only way to get it is to get people to talk about your site. That's where social media comes in.

ATTRACTING TRAFFIC WITH SOCIAL MEDIA

How to use social media to drive website traffic is worth a whole separate book (and more than a few have been written on the subject). Whatever your approach to social media is, you'll want to somehow integrate it with your WordPress site.

This, again, will probably fall to a plugin. "Going viral" may be the best thing that can happen to any small business Web page. But before you go viral, someone influential has to share your site in the first place. Plugins that place "Share this" buttons on your content pages make this just a little bit easier for your users.

A related type of plugin is the sort that will automatically repost your content to your own social media accounts. If you have a Facebook or Twitter account, for example, you can configure your WordPress site to automatically make a post to those networks every time you add new content to your site.

Many users won't actually take the trouble to visit your website independently. Reaching out to them on social media networks that present them with a constant stream of updates will help keep you connected to that audience.

Everything we've talked about here so far revolves around *organic* search results—the ones that come from people searching and surfing naturally. But there's another way to get found: paid advertising.

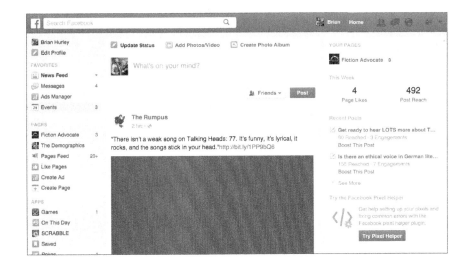

FIGURE 21

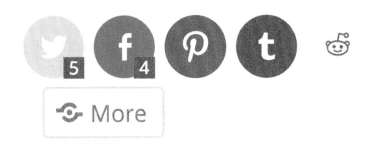

FIGURE 22

Increasingly, both social-media and Web-search companies are happy to take your money to improve your exposure to their users. There are also advertising networks that allow you to buy ad space on other websites—perhaps even your rivals'—to link back to your site.

Used judiciously, paid advertising can drive a considerable amount of traffic to your website. Here are some factors to keep in mind:

- It's surprisingly affordable, often costing only cents per click.

- Typically, you provide a budget for a specified time period.

- Bidding is done by keyword—market-driven systems auction off ad keywords according to demand at a given time.

- The more popular the keyword, the higher the price.

- Be careful to qualify your keywords. If you sell baseballs on your site, for example, you might think "baseball" would be a fine keyword to pull in traffic. But you'll get more people looking for baseball *scores* than looking to *buy* baseballs, and all those clicks you pay for will be a waste. Make your keywords specific to your product or service.

Getting found is a big challenge, and low traffic numbers may be discouraging at first. But time is the secret sauce for any of these methods for driving visitors to your site. You'll find that the longer you run the site, the greater your exposure will be. Your numbers will accelerate toward some natural plateau. Be patient and persistent and you *will* reach your audience.

WHAT'S SEO?

SEO basically comprises two parts:

- The first part is structural; it attempts to make your content easier for popular search engines (Google, Yahoo, Bing, and the like) to index using their automated Web-crawling tools.

- The second part is subject matter; it seeks to present content in such a way that the search engine will display it closer to the top of the list of results for a given search term.

WordPress itself, and to an even greater extent most themes, performs much of the structural optimization automatically. This optimization takes into account the following factors:

- URL structure; search engines like to see words related to the content, rather than random numbers or concatenated words, i.e. "http://example.com/purple-widgets" rather than "http://example.com/p745.html"

- Pages with valid and proper HTML syntax

- Title words with an appropriate emphasis

- Spurious code on the page and reducing it

- Speed! Some themes are better at this than others, but sites that load fast will be indexed more frequently and completely.

Other factors in search engine optimization are external, and you may not have much control over them. These include:

- Links to your website from other sites and the amount of traffic and search-engine authority those sites possess.

- Duplication of content between your website and other sites, leading to a lower ranking for both sites. This may be true even if they copied your site rather than the reverse.

- Personalized search results displayed to individuals on the basis of their own past search and browsing habits.

- Other undisclosed factors withheld by search-engine companies to prevent websites from gaming their system.

SELECTING KEYWORDS

Keywords and content are intimately related. Although keywords are words that you get to select and nominate to search engines as representative of your site, you're going to be graded: Google and other search engines compare your keyword selections with the actual frequency of words used on your site. This prevents nefarious websites from stuffing their keywords with popular phrases unrelated to the site, just to feature more prominently in search results.

Here are some tips for choosing keywords:

- Select keywords that will be used frequently in your site's content.

- Keywords don't have to be individual words; you can also use phrases. For example, "lemon cinnamon roll Seattle" is a keyword.

- Be as specific as possible.

- Look for alternate phrasings, such as "Seattle area lemon cinnamon rolls."

- Geographical keywords are as important as content keywords if you have a physical storefront.

- Audience profiles are valuable for providing keyword ideas. What words is your audience likely to use when searching for your products, services, or business?

- Use keyword-planning tools. By plugging in some rudimentary keywords, they can generate suggestions for more specific keywords that people are likely to use or are already using. See the Resources list on page 108 for links to some of these tools.

- Think outside the box. Most popular keywords will already be well-represented among competing sites. If you can find an apparently unrelated term that people are likely to use, that will give you an edge. Perhaps lemon cinnamon rolls go really well with orange juice, so "orange juice cinnamon roll" might be a "hidden" keyword to funnel customers to your site.

CREATE CONTENT

Content is king! Your ability to develop interesting, authentic, concise, and useful content about your business is a key factor in the success of your site for a number of reasons:

- Content determines how your site ranks in search engine results; the chances of someone clicking on your site from those results highly depends on the content.

- Social media buzz comes from attracting people to useful or interesting content on your site.

- Engagement with your audience depends on their interest in what you present. That, in turn, depends on how you present it to them.

Content is more than just words. Images, video, audio, and products can all be considered different sorts of content. At the end of the day, you need to create a combination of content that works to grab your audience and keep them interested long enough to accomplish your website's goals.

FIGURE 23

This emphasis on good content transcends the different types of business websites:

- If you're building a brochure-style website, the limited amount of content you post will be the sum total of how your business is judged by visitors.

- If you're creating an interactive site, your posts and comments will be the basis for customer reactions.

- If you're building an e-commerce site, how you describe and display your products will determine if anyone wants to buy them.

- If you're putting together a media site, you have to have content that trumps what your competitors can offer.

There are three basic ways to build content for your site:

1. Create it yourself.
2. Buy it from someone else.
3. Steal it!

The following sections explain these options in more detail.

ROLLING YOUR OWN CONTENT

Creating your own content may be the easiest and cheapest solution. But you need time and talent to make this option work. Your skills might also need to span the *entire* content spectrum. For example, if you're a great writer but can't compose a picture to save your life, you may still fall flat.

If you decide to create your own content, play to your strengths. If, as in the previous example, you write well but can't take decent pictures, then you will have to rely primarily on text to get your content across. You still need a variety of content types, but you can lean on your strong points.

Don't neglect to mine your staff for talent, too. Often, folks with strong customer-service or customer-relations skills can crank out content that your users will find appealing. Even in a relatively small business, you might find you have enough skills in house to cover the range of content required. Providing different perspectives from actual employees working in your business is also a great way to keep posts interesting and fresh.

Keeping content creation in-house offers other advantages as well. You can be more nimble in publishing content, and, presumably, you have a niche appeal that you can focus on. For example, you may not be the only bakery in town with a website now, but your cinnamon rolls have no competition!

But if, like a lot of small business owners, you're more interested in doing your job than writing about it, you'll need to find another way to get content for your website.

OUTSOURCING CONTENT CREATION

Since the Internet is so big and wonderful, you will find that you actually have a lot of options for outsourcing your content creation. But be careful! No one you hire is going to care about your business as much as you do. You'll still need to be a judge and gatekeeper. Buying blog posts from India at a penny a word is inexpensive, but you sacrifice quality.

There are a number of venues for hiring content creators, several of which are listed in the Resources section at the end of this book. But before turning to those sites, first consider hiring someone you know. Or perhaps your customer base can be a source of talent that's familiar with your products and industry. No one is more convincing than someone who already loves what you do.

FIGURE 24

GETTING YOUR USERS TO CREATE CONTENT

There's another option for content creation for certain types of small business sites: steal it!

Well, not really *steal* it. But for sites that are primarily about interaction and participation, your *customers* might prove to be the best source of content.

Forums and customer-service websites end up with a lot of content generated by users. If you create that kind of site, then your primary role may be to direct and edit that constant stream of information. For example, you might start a conversation by posting a question about baking cinnamon rolls. If you have the right audience, you'll probably get a flood of responses from intrigued amateur bakers.

Once the ball is rolling, you can step back and reach in occasionally to nudge the conversation in a certain direction or highlight information of particular importance by featuring it elsewhere, often creating the basis for the next conversation in the process. Think of Facebook: no one at Facebook headquarters spends time sitting around thinking up hot topics to post about. Their users are doing it all for them, all the time.

A variation on this technique is republishing information from elsewhere on the Web. Various plugins allow you to process and republish RSS feeds from other websites. (RSS stands for Really Simple Syndication; once again, plugins will be your solution if this is your approach.) However, make sure you give the appropriate credit for this content, and don't abuse this system.

With both approaches, you need to exercise some oversight and editorial control. You can get a lot of good content for almost nothing if you use this model correctly, but you can also get burned by posts that are outside your control.

For marketing or e-commerce sites, you'll probably go through this process of content creation only once or a few times a year. For just about every other type of site, more frequent updates are the norm. You might decide to use different labels for your site (articles, stories, etc.), but for the purposes of this discussion, let's just call it all "blogging"—which just so happens to be the subject of the next section.

TYPES OF SITES, TYPES OF CONTENT

MARKETING/BROCHURE: Creating content for a brochure-style site requires more up-front investment in time and resources than for other site types. You will be posting the sum total of your presentation all at once and leaving it up there, essentially unchanged, for the life of the site. So your presentation needs to be accurate, engaging, and search-optimized the day you hit the Publish button. It may be worth hiring a professional copywriter or marketing firm to work with you on this type of site.

INTERACTIVE: Content for customer-service or community-building sites is different from that of marketing sites in that much of it should come from the community itself. Your role with this type of site is to get the ball rolling rather than filling in all the blanks. You'll need content that asks questions or sparks conversations rather than providing all the answers.

E-COMMERCE: E-commerce–site content revolves around product descriptions and testimonials. You'll have to provide good images and clear, accurate representations of items you're selling. Additionally, you might provide comment or testimonial mechanisms for your satisfied customers to help you out—nothing sells a product like an ebullient buyer!

MEDIA: Media (a.k.a. informational) websites thrive on accuracy and frequent updates. You'll need to publish posts that are fresh and informative on at least a daily basis—or even more often than that. On the flip side, you'll have some leeway in post quality—since you can update rapidly, you can also make any necessary corrections quickly. And since older posts are supplanted by newer posts, mistakes won't sit at the top of your site like a dead salmon and stink up the place. They'll be pushed down and blissfully forgotten as newer and better posts supplant them.

BEING A GOOD BLOGGER

Blogging is probably what comes to mind when you think of WordPress, but hopefully you've come to understand that blogging is only one way to get your message out. Still, blogging has a number of advantages:

- It's perceived as a more casual type of writing than what's expected in brochures or product descriptions, so mistakes are more easily forgiven.
- The frequency of posts is an advantage both in SEO and audience interest. Search engines and people alike want to see what's new.
- The commitment level can be lower than with more formal publication styles.

But there are some drawbacks as well:

- Updates don't need to be constant, but they should be *consistent*; a blog that starts with a flurry of posts but then has no updates for a year signals bad things about your business.
- The ease of publishing can get you into trouble. Some sort of review and consideration has to be exercised to avoid accidentally posting offensive content. You don't want to go viral *that* way.

Consider blogging if:

- You have a steady stream of new information to release or interesting stories to tell about your business.
- You have an audience interested in viewing that content.
- You have a reliable, well-informed writer (or writers) to produce the posts.

KEEPING THE QUALITY CONTENT COMING

It can be difficult to avoid falling into a rut after you've talked about all the most interesting parts of your business. After all, there are only so many things you can say about cinnamon roll frosting.

A good place to look for topics is from your audience. Give them a way to offer feedback and ask them what they want to hear about from you. They will probably give you more ideas than you know what to do with.

BUYING CONTENT

Over the past decade, venues for hiring content creators have exploded along with the rest of the Internet. Elance, Odesk, and Scripted are only a few of the online marketplaces where you can quickly and easily hire freelance writers, illustrators, and photographers. Hundreds of hungry creative types are waiting to bid on your project right now.

Sites likes Constant Content and Ghost Bloggers come at the problem from a different angle. There, you can look through large catalogs of articles already written on a wide variety of subjects and buy publication rights for a fixed fee.

If you need pictures rather than text, sites like iStockphoto and Getty Images have thousands that you can buy rights for and download instantly.

Regardless of where you hire someone to produce your content, there are number of things to keep in mind to get good results:

LOOK FOR CANDIDATES WHO HAVE WORKED IN YOUR INDUSTRY BEFORE. You don't want to have to teach them everything from scratch.

STAY IN TOUCH! Outsourcing requires careful and constant supervision. Don't assume everything is going well—set up regular check-ins and reports.

WATCH OUT FOR PLAGIARISM AND COPYRIGHT ISSUES. Google will blacklist you in a heartbeat for copyright violations. Plagiarism checks are performed by some content mills, and you can do it yourself through sites like Plagscan.com.

BE CLEAR WHAT RIGHTS YOU'RE BUYING. If unique content is important to you (and it probably should be), make sure you're buying *unique* rights rather than *usage* rights.

Competitors and your industry are also sources for topics. What's new in the baking world? Someone is sure to find it fascinating.

The last thing you want your business website to do is to make it look like your business is dying. Unfortunately, this is exactly what happens when you start off by publishing a lot of content frequently and then trail off to pushing out only meager and sporadic updates. Pace yourself: make a schedule and stick to it.

The type of site you're running might offer a little more latitude for cyclical posting. If you have a media website, for example, it's only natural for information to come in waves.

Although publishing regularly is important, it's not *so* important that it trumps quality—you don't want an occasional gem to be buried in a pile of garbage. So don't allow an arbitrary schedule to force you to put out sub-standard content. If you find you can't keep up with your schedule and still create substantive, interesting content, cut back your schedule.

GET PAID

Since you're interested in creating a business website, it seems likely that, at some point, you're going to want to make some money off your site.

If you're creating a site solely for informational or marketing purposes, this will probably occur indirectly—your business will be boosted by financial transactions that happen outside the scope of the site itself. Increasingly, however, commerce happens directly on the Web. The promise of instant gratification and closing a sale without additional interactions are powerful motives for both businesses and consumers. Whatever business you're in, it behooves you to think about ways you could be selling your product or service directly via your website.

WordPress offers a number of solutions for businesses offering either products or services. There are themes and plugins that are designed specifically to create e-commerce sites in WordPress, and they tend to have features that fulfill a number of specialized requirements:

Templates for displaying products in various formats: For example, you may be able to create horizontal or vertical grids or take advantage of sorting and zooming options. Many solutions let you create product variants that allow a single basic product to be managed centrally but offered in a variety of sizes or colors.

Product inventory management: You enter details such as dimensions, shape, and descriptions for your products and upload a variety of pictures. The plugin can then automatically create detail pages for each product.

Payment calculations and transaction handling: Plugins allow you to choose shipping options and tax settings, which will then be automatically calculated for customers shopping from any locale. The plugins may also offer options for automatically integrating with various online payment processors such as PayPal, Google, and Amazon to make accepting payments easy. Alternatively, plugins are available for more traditional credit card–processing services.

Software integration: Many plugins are available to integrate your e-commerce sales directly with your regular business-accounting and inventory-management software. You won't have to double-enter data because it's automatically imported and synchronized.

Marketing campaign and coupon options: You can create discounts and e-mail coupons tailored to certain customers or products. These can often integrate with third-party e-mail newsletter services like MailChimp if you prefer to use those instead.

FIGURE 25

Affiliate management: Easily create affiliate networks of other websites that will sell your products. Affiliate software will track the sales, calculate the payments, and handle fulfillment options.

Online reviews: Your customers can easily rate and review your products directly on your site.

Reporting: Sales and browsing trends can be tracked so you can see which products are hot and which marketing efforts are paying dividends.

Not all plugins and themes are compatible with one another. This becomes more evident the more complex each of them becomes, so check the details before you pick them. Many of the most popular e-commerce plugins have a complete ecosystem of other plugins specially designed to complement or extend them.

If your products are specialized or virtual, make sure you find plugins that will support them. For instance, some plugins don't easily handle digitally downloadable products, while others specialize in them.

For simpler selling environments, you don't need to go to such trouble. If you have only a few products that are unlikely to change much over time or if you primarily provide services that aren't easy to represent as discrete units, you may find it easier to create listing pages manually. A simple PayPal or card-processing plugin without bells and whistles can do a fine job of letting you accept online payments.

COMMERCE IN THE CLOUD

Another alternative is to make use of a cloud-based e-commerce service. Commercial storefront services like Amazon's Webstore or Shopify can be set up without using WordPress at all. The features these services offer for tracking and managing your product listings are very advanced. Amazon's fulfillment options and your exposure to their huge marketplace may be reason enough to list products there.

However, your ability to customize and design your online store are greatly restricted by their templates and site paradigms. Also, because you're not completely in charge of the site, you may find yourself in an awkward position if their terms of service change in a way you don't like. It's not unheard of for companies to go out of business, either. If that happened to the only venue you had for sales, you would be left scrambling.

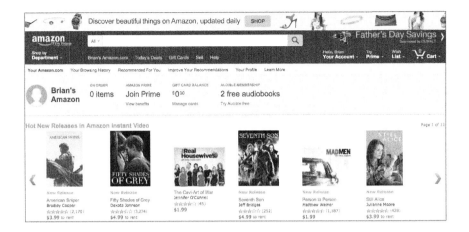

FIGURE 26

You can get all the advantages of using a cloud service while maintaining your independence by combining those services with your own site. You can use plugins to display your Amazon or Shopify listings directly on your WordPress site, retaining all the advantages of their cart and checkout systems, while retaining your ability to showcase your products exactly the way you want to. If Amazon booted you out tomorrow, you would simply have to find another back-end solution—not fun, but better than having to retrain your customers regarding where to look for your products.

You can also take advantage of such systems to integrate your support and knowledge base with your storefront, without actually having to build the storefront. To customers, everything appears to be on your site, even though the cloud e-commerce provider is doing all the heavy lifting of inventory management, payment processing, and possibly even fulfillment in the background on their own systems.

SALES SUCCESS

Online sales can be slow to take off, just as they can be for your brick-and-mortar storefront. But a big advantage of the online venue is that it costs next to nothing to operate while you're sitting around trying to figure out how to drive customers to it. So don't be quick to give up if your sales are slow initially. Take some time and come at it from another angle until you figure out the best strategy.

On the other end of that spectrum, be prepared for wild success. Your physical store is limited to some extent by physical constraints: there are only so many people in driving range and only so much floor space to pack them into. Sales can only be rung up only so fast. E-commerce has no such constraints. If you have a viral hit on your hands, half the Internet might place an order in a couple hours. The first few minutes, during which you become wildly rich, will be fun. The remainder, when disappointed customers vent their ire on social media after your inventory has evaporated, will be horrific.

It may be beyond your wildest dreams, but think up some contingency plans for coping with such success should it strike you. These strategies might include

- Having coupons ready to distribute to customers if you run out of inventory. If you have to turn them away, at least give them a reason to come back.

- Cannibalizing your other sales channels to fulfill website demand.

- Outsourcing some of your fulfillment to other vendors. It's possible to use Amazon, for instance, to hold stock and deal with much of the mechanics of fulfillment with almost no time to scale up.

- Raising your prices! This technique only requires typing in a few new numbers, after all. Selling out too fast might be a sign that you're charging less than the market will bear.

SELLING ADS

Selling advertising on your site is another option for making money. This is a decision that's fraught with complications and which isn't usually recommended for small business websites. After all, you're typically trying to market your own goods and services on your site, so devoting any of that precious screen real estate to hawking wares for someone else is just a distraction for potential customers.

But for certain types of sites, advertising may actually be part of your business model. If you're building a media website, for instance, advertising might become your primary revenue stream.

There are two ways to find advertisers for your site:

- Use an advertising network, such as Google's AdSense or Media.net.
- Approach potential advertisers and sell ad space directly.

Going with an advertising network is usually the easiest option. However, you'll sacrifice some cut of your potential revenues to the network operator, and you will typically lose some control over exactly what ads appear on your site.

Going directly to potential advertisers will probably work well for you if you have a niche site with an audience that falls into well-defined demographic slices. You can negotiate the terms of your deal more specifically than with an advertising network and keep all of the profits. However, you'll also have to go out and do the legwork of finding and dealing with the individual advertisers.

There are plugins available that make both options easy to integrate with your WordPress site. Google, in fact, offers a free AdSense plugin that not only makes displaying ads from their network easy, but also improves your site's integration with their Webmaster Toolset.

If you don't want to install a plugin for ads, you can use the basic WordPress text widget to insert and position the ad display codes.

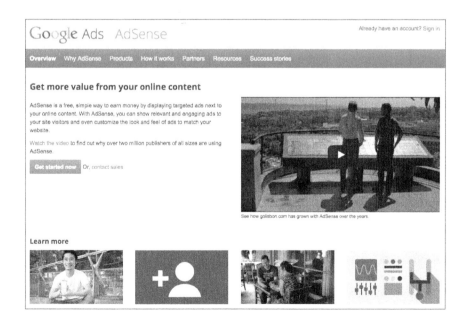

FIGURE 27

A SUPER-SIMPLE E-COMMERCE SITE IN EIGHT STEPS

1. On your Dashboard administration screen, go to Plugins and click Add New; then search for "simple e-commerce." One of your first results should be "WordPress Simple Ecommerce Shopping Cart Plugin—Sell products through PayPal." Click Install Now.

2. After the plugin has downloaded, click Activate Plugin. Once it has been activated, you'll see a new menu item on your Dashboard administration screen: Simple eCommerce. Click it.

3. Click Add/Edit Products. A screen will come up asking for details about your product. Go down the list and enter any information that's applicable. At a minimum, enter the name, a price, and a sales pitch. You can add variations (different colors or sizes), add a picture, and configure tax and shipping options, if you like. When you're finished, click Save. The newly entered product will appear in the Product list at the bottom of the page.

4. Now that you have a product for sale, you need some way for people to give you money for it. Under the Simple eCommerce plugin, click Settings.

5. Scroll down to Payment Gateway Settings. You'll see a box for entering a PayPal e-mail address and a checkbox for PayPal Standard Checkout. That's your only option with this simple, free system, but it's quick and easy. If you have an existing PayPal account, enter the e-mail address associated with it and click Save. If you don't have an account, you can skip this step for now.

6. Other settings available here allow you to configure currency, automatic thank-you e-mails, and display options for your storefront. You don't have to change any of those settings, but you can if you like.

7. Something sneaky has happened while you were doing all this: a whole new set of pages has been added to your site! Click Pages and you'll see them. You now have pages for Store, Cart, Checkout, and other commerce-related functions. On the Store page, click View.

8. Congratulations! Your product is now available for purchase. Doesn't it look great? If you entered a valid PayPal account in step 5, you can click "Add to Cart" and go through the checkout process to buy something from yourself. You'll get an e-mail anytime someone makes a purchase.

This plugin gives you many other options. For example, you can change which page the storefront appears on and customize appearance and behavior. The Reports page will track your sales and revenues and show you your product and category performance.

There are hundreds of similar e-commerce plugins, all with their own advantages and disadvantages. There's no penalty for trying out the free ones (most will want to sell you upgrades for more advanced options), but be careful to deactivate and remove pages created by older ones before testing new ones: there may be conflicts that prevent them from functioning correctly when installed simultaneously.

PART

3

GOING PUBLIC

You didn't go to all the trouble of building a website for your business only to have it sitting there, did you? Of course not. You want hits, traffic, eyeballs, sales. Here's how to get them.

INTERACT

You might want to use your WordPress website as a sort of virtual billboard, an online advertisement extolling your virtues and advantages to spectators who come across it. That is a valid choice for some businesses.

The real power of the Internet, though, is in connectivity and interaction. If you're not taking advantage of those qualities, you should take a close look at your online strategy. There are few businesses that won't benefit from more interaction with customers and potential customers.

A market is one big feedback loop, where customers give you money if they approve of your products and withhold it if they don't. Finding out *why* they do or don't is a challenge that interaction will help you overcome.

CREATING AND MANAGING COMMENTS

WordPress is built for this sort of conversation. A strong comment system is woven into the fabric of the software; you'll notice that Comments is one of the menu selections in the left column of your Dashboard administration screen. Every post and page on your site can be opened up to comments from users. By default, submitting feedback is as easy as typing text in the box at the bottom of a page and clicking Submit. Anyone can do it. The easier it is, the more people will do so.

Unfortunately, the easier it is, the more spammers will take advantage of it, too. Comment spam affects advertising and SEO. Spammers include links in the hope that search engines will increase the authority of other sites by making it seem as if you are linking to it from your site.

You can turn comments on and off on a per-page or per-post basis. To turn them off, head to the Pages or Posts administration dashboard, point your cursor at the title of the page or post you want to modify, click Quick Edit when it appears, and then uncheck "Allow comments." Oftentimes, pages have comments disabled, since comments can alter your keyword balance. Posts, however, usually allow comments. But you may decide on different standards for your site.

FIGURE 28

FIGURE 29

You can reply to or administer comments either on the pages where they're posted (you have to be logged in as the administrator) or centrally from the Comments administration screen, which provides a list of all comments made anywhere on your site. Let's take a look at this screen, because it's the easiest way to keep tabs on comments.

By default, WordPress asks for a name and e-mail address from commenters who don't have an account on your site or aren't logged in. They also have the option to include their own website address. There's no verification process for any of these values, so for all practical purposes, commenters are anonymous. The exception to that is that the IP address—a unique identifying number for the Internet connection they're using when they post the comment—is recorded.

You can see all of that information on the Comments administration screen. This can help you identify the commenter. You might find comments from many different names but only one IP address. This is usually a sign that someone with an agenda is masquerading as multiple users; that's bad.

Hover your cursor over one of the comments. You'll see that a number of menu options appear beneath it:

Unapprove will leave the comment in your system but remove it from public display. This is a good option if you want to hit "pause" on a conversation.

Reply allows you to type in a reply right from the Comments administration screen.

Quick Edit and *Edit* allow you to rewrite the user's comment. This is a powerful option for censoring comments, so be careful about using it; few things upset people more than having their words twisted. If you use this option to edit someone else's comment, it's customary to make a note in the comment's text indicating what edits you made and why.

Spam marks the comment as spam and removes it from display. This differs from Trash (described next) in that it helps your anti-spam system learn what you consider spam and trains it to automatically block such comments in the future.

Trash deletes the comment outright.

Comment spam is a huge red flag on a business website—it demonstrates a lack of attention that immediately discredits the website in the eyes of users. Use an anti-spam plugin like Akismet to help manage this, but stay on top of your comments personally, too!

To the right of the comment body, you can see the post or page it was made on; click this to visit it directly if you want to see the context behind the comment. There is also a small bubble with a number in it showing how many comments, total, that post or page has received. This helps you keep track of what's got people talking.

You can customize how your comments system works. To do so, click the Settings menu on the Dashboard administration screen and select the Discussion panel. There you'll find options for controlling how the Comment system works and how comments are displayed:

- You can require users to have an account on the site and be logged in to comment. This reduces spam but might also reduce legitimate feedback, particularly if you don't take the time to create a good user-registration system.

- You can require approval for comments. If you get a lot of comments, this can flood your inbox and create a lot of extra work.

- There are options for flagging or blacklisting comments based on their contents. Akismet does a much better job of this with a lot less work, but you can try to do it manually as well.

- You can control the Avatar system, which shows a small picture next to comments to identify the commenter.

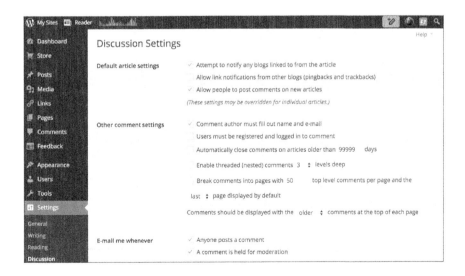

FIGURE 30

You may not want to use the comment system to hear from your customers. It takes time to do it properly and is susceptible to abuse. And failure to respond to comments or questions can be perceived as a sign that your business isn't serious. If you don't have the resources to monitor comments and reply to them, think about disabling comments. You don't want to make it look like no one's home!

CREATING A CONTACT FORM

A more private and easily managed option than contacts is a contact form. You can respond more selectively to these messages, which send an e-mail to the address of your choosing. If you fall behind or fail to respond to one of these messages, it's not immediately obvious to every single person who views your site (although you'll probably irritate at least one potential customer).

To use a contact form, you'll need to download a plugin. As usual, there are many options, but let's pick a random free one called (creatively) Contact Form:

1. Go to the Plugins menu and click Add New. Search for and install the Contact Form plugin.

2. Once it's installed, click Activate Plugin. You'll then see Contact Form in your Plugins list. Click Settings.

3. The required settings are pretty basic: either pick a user to have the form mailed to or put in a separate e-mail address. You can find many more options in the Additional Settings category (and if you buy the Pro version, even *more* under Appearance), but none are required.

4. Pick a post or page to include the contact form on and go into its visual editor. Paste "[contact_form]" (without the quotation marks) into the editor, then click Update.

5. Go view the page directly. You should see a basic form where you pasted the code asking the user to fill in their name, e-mail address, a subject, and the message text.

Anyone can fill in those fields and click Submit, and the message will be sent to the e-mail address you specified in the settings.

MAKE FRIENDS

WordPress is a kind of village. You're not the only one out there building a website home for your business. There are houses going up all around your online neighborhood, and a constant clatter of virtual hammers and yelling cyber-carpenters fills the electronic air.

As a sprawling open-source software project with nearly unlimited options for customization, not to mention adoption comprising almost a quarter of the Web, there are a lot of people and businesses involved either centrally or peripherally with WordPress. You, now, are one of them.

It's to your advantage to make connections within this community. Because both WordPress and many of its extensions are free, sometimes the best support options are other WordPress users. Developers who have already contributed their time and effort to coding something free aren't always available to answer your questions for nothing, too. Even when they are, they may have a limited familiarity with the specific combination of plugins and themes you're using.

However, WordPress is used in so many places and for so many purposes that there's almost certainly some other business owner out there who has already built the same sort of site you're trying to create. They've already tripped over all the obstacles and found all the hidden gotchas. They under-stand your frustration and will probably be willing to help you through it. You just need to get out there and connect with them.

You will find a separate community congregating around any popular theme or plugin provider. As you progress through building your site, you'll probably stumble across many of these. In time, you might find them more congenial and useful than the larger WordPress community. They tend toward more specialized uses and more advanced questions.

When you're first starting out, you're best off dipping your toes into the shallow end. You'll find that at the site where the software lives: WordPress.org.

THE WORDPRESS FORUMS

The WordPress.org Support forums are the heart and soul of the WordPress community. There, you can find everyone from expert developers who have been involved from the very beginning to rank amateurs. There are millions of posts going back more than a decade.

With such history, it may be difficult for you to come up with a question that hasn't been posed before. There may be no such thing as a stupid question, but there are an awful lot of questions that have already been answered a hundred times in every possible way. The polite thing to do before posing your own query is to make a cursory search of the site to see if it has already been answered. To do so, just type a brief summary of your question ("How do I install new widgets?") in the Search box in the upper right corner of the WordPress.org site. It doesn't hurt to do a Google search, too.

If you don't find the answer to your question, you need to register for a WordPress.org forum account before you can post your question:

1. Go to WordPress.org/support.

2. In the upper right part of the page, click the Register button.

3. On the screen that appears, you can choose to subscribe to the WordPress newsletter. It's not really necessary since most of the information it contains will already show up on your Dashboard in the News widget, but if you prefer a copy in your inbox, go ahead and check the Subscribe box here.

4. Fill in a username and e-mail address where requested. You aren't required to provide any of the other information, but it's a good idea to do so; some of those details may help others who are trying to help you.

5. Click Register and you're done! A validation e-mail should show up shortly.

   Creating a forum account allows you to:

- Post questions and comments in the forums.

- Keep track of conversations of interest. Once you're logged in, you can "subscribe" to a thread so that you'll automatically be updated of any new comments when they appear.

- Mark topics for future reference. You'll be able to mark a conversation as a "favorite" so you can refer back to it in the future without searching.

- Tag forum topics just as you can tag posts on your own site, so they're easier to find in future searches.

Community participation is a two-way street. At first you'll probably have more questions than answers. That's natural. In time, you'll find that you have developed a little bit of WordPress expertise and you'll start to see questions that you know the answers to! When that happens, give a little back. Go browse through and answer a few posts that you can help with. In addition to feeling swell about yourself, you might learn some new things about topics you're already familiar with. The discussion explaining *why* certain solutions are better than others will improve your understanding of the system you're building.

The forums are not purely about support or even questions and answers. There's also discussion and feedback. Because WordPress uses a community-driven development process, your voice matters. Want a feature that hasn't been added yet? Something driving you nuts in the way the Dashboard administration screen is laid out? Post in the forums and join the clamor for change!

FIGURE 31

The Requests and Feedback forum provides you with direct access to the people developing the software. Don't waste the opportunity to ask for what you want or to say "thanks" for a feature you particularly appreciate. Developers are people, too!

If you're shy and more interested in consuming information than participating in a conversation, the forums are still beneficial. Lurking can be almost as useful as posting.

And if the WordPress online forums don't quite work for you, there's also a forum for organizing in-person meetups. You can find other WordPress users in your area and get together with them out in the real world for commiseration or assistance.

WORDCAMP

Another option for real-world WordPress gatherings is WordCamp.org, a community-organized series of WordPress conferences that are happening around the world all the time.

WordCamp conferences work like any other conference: they sell tickets, offer keynote presentations, and feature breakout sessions where presenters dive into detail on a variety of topics of interest to WordPress developers and users. If you attend one, you'll not only have the opportunity to learn directly from the presentations, but also to network and make connections with other nearby WordPress users.

If you can't make it to WordCamp, check out WordPress.tv, where videos from many of the presentations from WordCamps around the world are archived. Other training videos are also available there. And, in the grand WordPress tradition, you can submit your *own* videos for inclusion on the site if WordPress training-video production happens to be your thing.

COMMUNITY BEYOND WORDPRESS

All this feel-good community building doesn't have to end at the WordPress gates. For many of the same reasons that it's a good to participate in the WordPress community, it's also a good idea to be a part of your business community.

The form this participation takes depends a lot on the business you're in. Some industries are, by nature, more congenial than others. Yours might be competitive and cutthroat, or it might already have well-organized trade groups with social media accounts, websites, and meetups.

Whatever you have in common with other WordPress business users in general, you'll have even *more* in common with others from your industry. The way you end up building your website might result in some competitive advantage. However, it might also follow some fairly natural blueprints for industry best practices. If you can find someone who has built such a site before and is willing to provide advice, you can avoid a lot of stumbling around.

In this sense, there's a sort of Golden Rule aspect to connecting with similar businesses: a little ethical cooperation is likely to benefit everyone.

You connect with other people in your industry using the same channels you use for connecting with customers.

- "Friend" your competitors on Facebook.

- Follow their Twitter accounts.

- Give them a shout-out on your own site in a blog post. Referencing industry news or a competing product can be terrific fodder for new blog conversations.

- Set up an RSS feed to republish select content from industry websites.

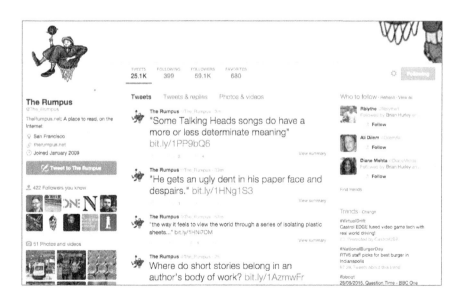

FIGURE 32

All this can improve your image with your customers by making you appear confident and plugged in. It also helps you by imbuing your site with industry authority in search-engine rankings. Modern search-ranking algorithms have a sophisticated view of the Internet. Connections between sites within certain keyword realms are part of their analyses. So if you link to, and are linked from, other sites that are highly ranked in the same keyword branches, then your website's ranking will tend to rise.

MEASURE YOUR SUCCESS

There's only one way to know if you're meeting your website goals: metrics on which to judge them and receive feedback. Do you recall your SMART goals? Remember what the M stands for? That's right: measurable.

So how do you measure your goals? In part, it depends on what they are, and the results may seem obvious. For example, if you were trying to increase your online sales and you didn't have any before, then the first dollar that comes in via your website is a sign of success!

But your goals and the progression you follow to attain them probably won't be so easy to assess. Selecting and monitoring the metrics appropriate to achieving those goals is key to succeeding.

SELECTING YOUR METRICS

Since you are a businessperson, you're no stranger to metrics. Some of the common metrics you can use to measure your website's success are the same as those you use to evaluate your business. Costs, revenues, and profits are all as valid yardsticks for websites as they are for any other part of your business.

Computers thrive in a data-rich environment, and you'll find that websites come with a thicket of other performance metrics. Even a cursory glance at a basic website-analytics package reveals a bewildering array of strangely labeled numbers: hits, uniques, page views, bounces, sessions, durations, and every combination of the above. If you're not steeped in Web lore, they may all seem like random numbers with no practical application to your goals.

In fact, some of those numbers are probably *vital*. The trick is to figure out which ones to pay attention to and which to filter out.

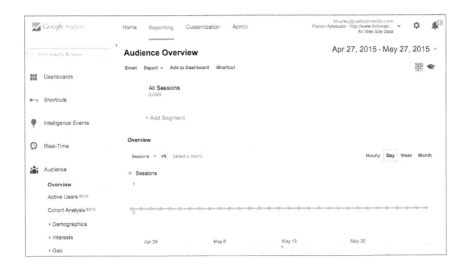

FIGURE 33

A good analytics package can help you do exactly that. But first you have to learn a little bit about what the numbers they provide mean. Here are some of the most common and important metrics:

Users or unique users: Represents a single visitor to your site, even if they make multiple visits.

Visits or sessions: The total number of visits to your site. This number best represents your overall traffic level.

Page views: The total number of pages or posts viewed during all visits to your site.

Bounce rate: The rate at which website visitors view a single page on your site and then click away without interacting. This is an inverse measure of your initial appeal and relevance to visitors.

Session length and pages per session: These are separate metrics that tell you about the same thing: how long users are spending on your site and how many pages they view during each visit. This tells you how interesting or "sticky" your site is.

Source: How users found your site; this could be through search results or social media or by directly typing your address into their browsers.

Exits: How many users left the site from a particular page. Pages with a lot of exits (unless it is a checkout page) often have something wrong with them.

There are countless permutations and derivations of these basic metrics. They can also be sliced narrowly, so that you can find the numbers for a specific page on your site. Advanced analytics systems can even tell you how people navigate through your site from page to page and even where on the page they are most likely to click. They can also tell you how your site is doing and provide more details about your users, including:

- Page load speed
- Pages that generate errors
- What pages are linked to from which outside sites
- Browser language settings
- Geographic location
- Operating system or mobile-device type

Many analytics packages also work with e-commerce or advertising systems. These can tell you which ads generate the best results and which products are most popular, as well as break down your revenue-per-product variant.

If you're a real data nerd, you can pull all that information together in ways that are a little spooky. For example, you might find that all your sales of XXL red T-shirts are coming from two iPhone users living in a small town in rural Georgia. Even spookier, many packages will give you that information in real time. You can watch one of those guys on your site *right now*. (Do they match your audience profile? If so, goal achieved!)

Any of these metrics might have varying levels of relevance to you depending on your website's type:

Marketing/brochure: Your total number of users is probably going to be most important. You might want to know what pages they are looking at, to gauge interest, but if what you are most interested in is just getting your information out there, then what's important is how many people see it.

Interactive: Stickiness is most important for interactive sites. You'll want to pay attention to session time and pages per session. Geography might also be important.

E-commerce: Sales data will obviously be important, but you'll likely also want to track *how* people are getting to the products that are selling—or where they're falling out of your sales "funnel" for products that aren't doing well.

Media: Stickiness is also a factor for media sites, but what will probably interest you more is the source where your traffic is coming from. This will help you know your audience and tailor your content.

You probably hear about "hits" all the time, but that measurement is widely misunderstood and probably doesn't have much relevance today. Some analytics packages don't even report that number, and even if they do, you should probably ignore it.

PICKING AN ANALYTICS PACKAGE

You have three options for obtaining detailed site metrics:

1. Install an analytics plugin.
2. Use analytics provided by your hosting service.
3. Use a third-party, Web-based analytics service.

If you search for "analytics" in the WordPress plugin repository, most of the plugins you'll see listed are really just connectors for Google Analytics. (More about that in a minute.) Other plugins generate statistics based on user interactions with your site. This might be sufficient, but there are some limitations—for example, they can only build numbers based on what happens on your site itself.

Many website providers include some sort of external analytics system as a part of your hosting package. Although some of these are powerful and fully featured, most are rudimentary at best. With some hosting providers, however—WordPress.com is the prime example—you *can't* use third-party services like Google, so this is what you'll be stuck with.

As a practical matter, the best option in the third-party category is Google Analytics. There are a number of cloud-based analytics systems that can integrate with and monitor your site. But the reality is that a significant chunk of all Internet browsing starts with a Google search. Consequently, Google is in the best position to track and report on Web-browsing characteristics.

You'll need a Google Analytics account before you can get started. Here's how to get one:

1. If you already have a Google account, you're halfway there. If not, go sign up for one at https://accounts.google.com/SignUp. You should be using Google's Webmaster Tools to help manage SEO anyway.

2. Visit http://google.com/analytics. You'll be asked to sign up for an Analytics account. Pick the option called Access Google Analytics.

3. You'll have to give your account a name; use your business name if you like. Enter your website's URL. You can include the "www" part or leave it off, but you'll be locked into that choice, so pick whichever you prefer. Make sure to include a trailing slash in the address, like so: www.example.com/.

4. The industry category and time-zone settings are for your convenience but otherwise unimportant.

5. Click the Get Tracking ID button. You'll be prompted to agree to the terms of service, then you'll be presented with a few lines of gibberish. Copy and save this text—you'll need it later. Make sure you get all of it and *don't* alter it.

Tracking ID

UA-63531709-1

Website tracking

This is the Universal Analytics tracking code for this property. **To get all the benefits of Universal Analytics for this property, copy and paste this code into every webpage you want to track.**

This is your tracking code. Copy and paste it into the code of every page you want to track.

```
<script>
(function(i,s,o,g,r,a,m){i['GoogleAnalyticsObject']=r;i[r]=i[r]||function(){
(i[r].q=i[r].q||[]).push(arguments)},i[r].l=1*new Date();a=s.createElement(o),
m=s.getElementsByTagName(o)[0];a.async=1;a.src=g;m.parentNode.insertBefore(a,m)
})(window,document,'script','//www.google-analytics.com/analytics.js','ga');

ga('create', 'UA-63531709-1', 'auto');
ga('send', 'pageview');

</script>
```

FIGURE 34

Now that you have the tracking code, you can pick any of the available Google Analytics plugins and install them. In the settings for the plugin, you'll be asked to provide the Tracking ID you copied earlier. Enter it *exactly*.

Within 24 hours, you'll be able to go back to the Google Analytics site and starting poking around in your tracking data.

USING YOUR METRICS

Once you have all this analytics magic hooked up and spitting out numbers, you'll need to integrate the information into your feedback loop. Knowing the numbers is the first step. Finding the knobs to make them go in the right direction is second.

The specific numbers you want to see will depend on the type of site you're running and your goals for the site. Almost every site operates using something called a *conversion funnel*. The funnel describes the steps the ideal user will follow in order to fulfill the goal you have for them. By monitoring the metrics that track users through this funnel, you can tell what aspects of the site need to be altered to meet those goals.

For example, an e-commerce site funnel might look something like this:

- Enter the site on the home page.
- Click a menu category of products of interest.
- Click a specific product on the category page.
- Read a detailed description of the product.
- View images of the product.
- Buy it!

Your site metrics will show you what's happening at each of those steps (typically, each will occur on a separate page). Inevitably, you will see some drop-offs at each step (which is what makes the funnel shape)—users may realize they don't like the look of the item or read in the description that it wasn't exactly what they wanted.

But perhaps you see a steep drop at one particular step. That's a sign there's something wrong there; either you're presenting something in an unappealing way or you haven't correctly qualified people further up the funnel.

Even if there is nothing obviously wrong with the traffic pattern, you almost certainly want to widen the funnel to shuffle more users through. Either way, it's time to start making some changes.

This is a good time to look back to your audience profiles. What exactly is not meeting their expectations or needs so that they drop out of the funnel at a given point? Either the profile is inaccurate or something about that page isn't clicking.

Another possibility is that the funnel itself is poorly constructed. You might need to tweak how the site is organized. For example, presenting the product picture before the description might engage people better.

You can make these changes one at a time (not all at once!) and wait to see how they affect the numbers. This will take some time and restrict you to making changes in isolation—if you try two different things at the same time on the same page, then you won't know which one shifted the numbers.

There is a better alternative, though: A/B testing (a.k.a. multivariate testing).

A/B testing involves using the power of your server to offer multiple versions of your site simultaneously. Alternating visitors to your site will see different versions of pages that you provide. Each of them will have a unique experience; they won't be aware of the other versions that are being shown. Their statistics will be tracked separately and reflect their response only to the particular revision they see.

As this is happening, the analytics package breaks out these numbers so that you can compare the metrics from the different versions. You'll see almost immediately which performs better.

Google Analytics offers the ability to perform A/B testing free, which is another advantage of selecting it as your analytics package. But it can be complicated to set up properly for nontechnical users.

A variety of plugins are available (for a fee) that will either integrate and automate A/B testing in conjunction with Google Analytics or will provide the test mechanism and resulting statistics independently.

FINAL TIPS FOR SUCCESS

CONTENT IS KING! From good content will flow all manner of popularity and success. There is no substitute. Post often, post accurately, post interestingly.

MAKE FRIENDS. Strike up conversations and you'll find that some of them lead back to your site.

SOLICIT FEEDBACK. If you want customers to comment or review your products or website, make sure you ask them. If you want a link from another website, e-mail the site's owner.

LIVE AND DIE BY SOCIAL NETWORKING. For a lot of sites these days, Facebook generates as many hits as Google does, and the customers it brings you tend to be better qualified and more interested than those from search engines.

BUY WEB-BASED ADVERTISING. Although you have to pay for this service and many of the hits will be of poor quality, you'll get exposure far past what your organic results will generate. Consider purchasing social network ads in addition to conventional ads.

DON'T FORGET TO TELL PEOPLE ABOUT YOUR SITE OFFLINE, TOO! Generate a QR code to link directly to your site and post it in your place of business. Print your website address on flyers and business cards. Make sure your mom knows your URL and recites it at her next book club meeting.

STAY SAFE

Any software that makes up almost a quarter of the Internet is going to be a big target for hackers. Discovery of a single vulnerability in WordPress can expose thousands of sites to compromise.

WordPress hasn't been immune to big security breaches. Incidents in 2011 and 2013 were splashed all over the international news.

Attacks like this are a reality of operating a website today. They're impossible to avoid, regardless of the system that you use, but they're not impossible to beat.

Hollywood has conditioned us to dread faceless, untouchable, omniscient hackers. Reality is more mundane. Most compromises are exploited by massive botnets, networks of thousands of already-compromised computers that employ unsophisticated attacks that succeed largely due to brute force of numbers.

The hackers who create these botnets aren't superhuman. In nearly every case, they are exploiting vulnerabilities that have already been discovered and fixed or that exist only because of bad habits on the part of site administrators. Consequently, the steps to basic Internet security with WordPress are the same as for any software and are easy to follow:

1. Change your administrative username (by default, it's "admin") and password.

2. Use a long, secure password with mixed cases, symbols, and numbers.

3. Change your password regularly.

4. Install any updates as rapidly as is practical.

5. Uninstall any plugins or themes that you're not using.

6. Back up your site regularly.

Although these steps are rudimentary, a surprising number of people don't follow them. You might think that you aren't a target. For example, say your site doesn't take or keep credit card information and you don't store any trade secrets or private customer info on the site. Why would hackers even bother?

Forbes ▾   New Posts   Most Popular   Lists   Video   10 Stocks to Buy Now   [Search]

4/13/2013 @ 2:56AM   70,617 views

Wordpress Under Attack: How To Avoid The Coming Botnet

Our continuing coverage

Humanizing
DATA

+ Comment Now   + Follow Comments

Anthony Wing Kosner
Contributor

FOLLOW

Quantum of Content and
Innovations in user
experience
full bio →

Opinions expressed by Forbes
Contributors are their own

LEARN MORE

SEAGATE

27
COMMENTS

+ Follow Comments

WordPress is easy. That's why people like it. It's quick to set up a simple site. It's easy
to manage large amounts of content. It's easy to add functionality without having to
know how to code php because there is such a large developer community that makes
tons of free plugins.

FIGURE 35

This attitude fundamentally misreads some of the realities for hackers today:

- First, since they are using botnets, it costs them nothing to attempt to hack as many sites as possible. It's relatively rare these days for a hacker to target a site like yours *specifically*. There's no need to—it's all automated. You're just getting caught up in a big net.

- Second, nefarious uses for compromised websites can extend well beyond what your good-natured, law-abiding imagination can come up with. Your site might not collect customer information. But there's nothing stopping a hacker from taking control, *pretending* to be your business, and soliciting information from your customers.

Another popular trick is to take over a website like yours and infect it with a virus that can, in turn, infect the computers that visit the site and compromise any private information from those computers.

So, just because you don't think your website is an appealing target for hackers doesn't mean it's safe. Don't take chances.

FIGURE 36

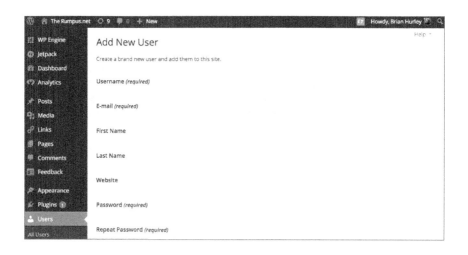

FIGURE 37

Fortunately, WordPress itself is pretty secure these days. The open nature of the development process ensures that many eyes review the code and many developers are available to fix any issues that are uncovered.

A more common route for compromises in WordPress is through plugins. Anyone can develop one, and so the quality of them varies greatly. Because the number of users and developers involved with any given plugin is a lot lower than the total number of WordPress users, there is less scrutiny. This leads to vulnerabilities that may be significant and hard to detect and patch.

Plugins can be a security hole in your site, but they can also provide a strong fence. A number of security-focused plugins are available to help secure your site. They can do everything from checking your password strength to scanning your server for file and database vulnerabilities to dynamically blocking detected hacking attempts from outside. These can provide a good backstop to basic site-security practices.

ACCESS CONTROL

Unless you run a particularly small business, you'll probably have more than one person work on your website. You should *not* let everyone use your administrator account. The more people who have that password, the greater the odds it will be leaked.

There's also the very real possibility of accidents. The site administrator can do anything from installing new plugins to deleting old ones. If the person using that account isn't careful, they can accidentally unravel your whole site with a few misplaced clicks.

Instead of sharing one account, create a separate account for each user. You can do this through the Users administration panel:

1. On the left side of the Dashboard administration screen, click Users.

2. Click Add New.

3. Fill in the Username, E-mail, and Password fields; everything else is optional. *Don't* check the box to send the password to the user via e-mail. Instead, give it to them in person or over the phone to be safe.

4. Choose an option from the Role drop-down menu. The role you assign controls their ability to manage the site. Give them the least amount of access they'll need to do their job:

   Administrators have full control of the site.

   Editors can publish and manage posts, including posts by other users.

   Authors can publish and manage only their own posts.

   Contributors can write and manage their own posts, but not publish them.

   Subscribers can comment on posts.

   Custom roles can also be created to combine various permissions.

   By restricting users to roles suitable to the tasks they'll perform on the site, you dramatically limit your exposure to either accidental or intentional disruptions.

DENIAL OF SERVICE

There's another category of attack against which WordPress can offer no defense: Denial of Service (DoS).

A DoS attack is generated by external computers (usually a large number of them; a variant is called a Distributed Denial of Service attack, or DDoS) that all attempt to connect to your site simultaneously. None of the individual attempts are illegitimate, but when combined, the traffic can overwhelm your server's capacity.

There's no risk of lost data or compromise from a DDoS attack, but that's little comfort if your business site is out of commission.

If you happen to find yourself on the wrong end of a DoS attack, you'll probably have to work with your hosting provider. Since a skilled DoS doesn't look much different from a really good traffic day, you'll need professional help.

KEEP UP WITH NEW DEVELOPMENTS

One key to keeping your business website safe and secure is keeping your software patched to the most current version. According to the Center for Strategic and International Studies, 75% of all security breaches are caused by exploiting vulnerabilities in software that the manufacturer has already fixed . . . but which the company *using* the software hadn't updated.

Fortunately, WordPress makes it extraordinarily easy to stay up-to-date. WordPress's Dashboard administration screen takes care of most of the heavy lifting of keeping you informed:

- If a new WordPress version is available, a notice will appear with an update link right at the top of the screen.
- Other updates are available under the Home administration menu in the left-hand column.
- Themes or plugins that have updated versions available will notify you by displaying a notice in their respective menus. An orange circle with the number of updates available will show up in the left-hand menu column.
- Patches for plugins and WordPress may not play nicely together, so it's a good idea to check details before installing updates, particularly if you use complex or uncommon plugins.
- It's a smart practice to create a test site that's a duplicate of your main website and test new patches there first.

The Dashboard administration screen also keeps you up-to-speed with what's going on in the WordPress world in general. In the Screen Options menu near the top right of the Dashboard, make sure the box next to WordPress News is checked. That way, every time you log into the Dashboard, you'll find a News box on display with headlines about WordPress developments, problems, or other items of interest. Click any of them to get more details.

BACKUPS

The final aspect of security to consider is making backups. A good, recent backup is your only option if all else fails.

Most hosting providers have some sort of rudimentary backup capability. These are usually inadequate, and you'll need to supplement them with your own efforts.

There are two components of a WordPress site that have to be backed up in order to be able to restore the site completely:

Files: The files that make up the code and pages of the site can usually be downloaded from your hosting manager or a File Transfer Protocol (FTP) client.

Database: The database that contains all the settings for the site and most of your content has to be backed up via a separate process, usually using a tool provided by your host, and then stored safely somewhere.

For an effective backup, you need a regular process for taking those two components and storing them somewhere *other* than the server that hosts the site. Keep security in mind when you pick a storage site! Any hackers who find your site backup laying around on a USB stick on your receptionist's desk, for example, just saved themselves a whole lot of hard work breaking into your site the old-fashioned way.

Apart from being safe, the other important aspect of your storage site is that it be someplace where you can get at it quickly if necessary.

The frequency of your backups will depend on your site's type and frequency of publication. If you put up new content only once per week, then you can get away with weekly backups; more frequent ones would be a waste of time. However, sites that have a lot of user interaction or that publish many times per day might back up *hourly*. Every minute that passes since the last backup is a window for losing data that has been created in the interval.

You will probably want to save a *series* of backups instead of keeping only the most recent one. Certain insidious problems of corruption or infection can sneak into backups unnoticed. If you discover the problem later, you'll have no good backup to restore. Instead, you can adopt a rotation scheme to keep sets of backups. Grandfather-father-son is a safe and time-tested scheme:

1. Create a full backup every day, replacing the set from the same day of the previous week.
2. Each Friday, set aside that day's backup and keep it until the same Friday of the following month.
3. The last Friday of each month, set aside that day's backup and keep it until the following year.

This scheme gives you a daily backup with fallback sets available from as far back as a year ago if necessary and more recent sets from each week and month. This provides more depth than most businesses will ever need and is fairly simple to implement.

GLOSSARY

API: Application Programming Interface; a method for connecting programs or websites together.

AVATAR: A visual representation or picture that may be selected to appear beside a user or author comment on a blog.

BLOG: From "weblog," a form of online diary.

BROCHURE WEBSITE: A type of website that is mostly static and used for marketing purposes.

BUSINESS-CARD SITE: See "brochure website."

CONTENT MANAGEMENT SYSTEM (CMS): A software program for storing and organizing various types of content, from text to images to video.

CONTENT MILL: A company that provides writers or photographers or content available for licensed display; usually inexpensive.

DEVELOPER: A programmer who works on themes or plugins.

HOSTING PROVIDER: A company that runs servers and leases services to operate websites for customers.

INTRANET: A private Internet for company employees and business associates.

KEYWORD: A word or phrase that is representative of the content of a particular page or post.

MULTISITE: A feature of WordPress that allows it to run multiple websites with a single server and administrative interface.

SEARCH ENGINE OPTIMIZATION (SEO): A process for improving site ranking in search-engine results by tailoring website structure and content so it's preferred by search algorithms for selected keywords.

SITEMAP: A digital representation of a website's pages and layout.

SOCIAL MEDIA: Sites such as Facebook and Twitter where users primarily interact with one another.

SPAM: Unsolicited comments posted as advertisements for third-party services or products or to increase other websites' SEO.

RESOURCES

PLANNING/DESIGN

Browserling: https://www.browserling.com
Tests various browsers against your website; free but slow.

BrowserStack: http://www.browserstack.com
Another web browser test site—fast, but requires a subscription.

Google AdWords Keyword Planner: https://adwords.google.com
/keywordplanner
Lets you search for relevant keywords for your site and see their search popularity.

Google Webmaster Tools: https://www.google.com/webmasters
Take control of your site in Google's listings by enrolling here.

Keyword Planner: http://keywordtool.io
Another keyword-analysis tool.

WordPress Official Showcase: https://wordpress.org/showcase
Examples of notable WordPress site designs.

PLUGINS

All in One SEO Pack: https://wordpress.org/plugins/all-in-one-seo-pack
Plugin to assist with search engine optimization for your site.

Akismet: http://akismet.com
Cloud-based, anti-spam filtering service.

Contact Form 7: https://wordpress.org/plugins/contact-form-7
A simple but powerful plugin that allows you to create e-mail contact forms for your site.

Google XML Sitemaps: https://wordpress.org/plugins
/google-sitemap-generator
Creates a digital diagram of your website so search engines can more easily index it.

JetPack: http://jetpack.me
Offers various tweaks, widgets, optimizations, statistics, and security features.

WooCommerce: http://www.woothemes.com/woocommerce
A popular e-commerce plugin with free and paid variants.

Woo Themes: http://www.woothemes.com
Woo develops many themes and plugins that work well together.

WordPress Simple eCommerce: https://wordpress.org/plugins
/simple-e-commerce-shopping-cart
A basic, free plugin that allows the direct sale of sites or services via your website.

WP Robots.txt: https://wordpress.org/plugins/wp-robots-txt
Allows you to specify parts of your site that you don't want indexed by search engine crawlers.

Yoast: https://yoast.com
Similar to Woo Themes, Yoast is a large plugin developer with a variety of services.

SEARCH ENGINE OPTIMIZATION

Various search engine companies publish guides to boosting your site to rank in their indexes. It's valuable to get this information directly from the source.

Google SEO Starter Guide: http://static.googleusercontent.com
/media/www.google.com/en/us/webmasters/docs
/search-engine-optimization-starter-guide.pdf

Bing Webmaster SEO Guidelines: http://www.bing.com/webmaster/help
/webmaster-guidelines-30fba23a

Search Engine Watch: http://searchenginewatch.com
Site dedicated to monitoring and reporting news on SEO and search.

CUSTOM CONTENT

Custom content providers connect you with freelancers who can produce graphics or text based on your specifications for a fixed fee or hourly rate.

Textbroker: https://www.textbroker.com

Elance: https://www.elance.com

Scripted: https://scripted.com

Upwork: https//www.upwork.com

PACKAGED CONTENT

Packaged content providers allow you to purchase rights to previously written articles or existing graphics for display on your site.

Constant Content: https://www.constant-content.com

Ghost Bloggers: http://www.ghostbloggers.net

Getty Images: http://www.gettyimages.com

iStockPhoto: http://www.istockphoto.com

PLAGIARISM DETECTORS

Be sure to check your purchased content for plagiarism! Search engines will punish you if it appears that you stole content from another site.

Dupli Checker: http://www.duplichecker.com

PlagScan: http://www.plagscan.com

HOSTING PROVIDERS

BlueHost: http://www.bluehost.com/wordpress

DreamHost: http://www.dreamhost.com/wordpress-hosting

HostGator: http://www.hostgator.com/apps/wordpress-hosting

WordPress.com: https://wordpress.com

WordPress.org's recommended provider list: https://wordpress.org/hosting

PAYMENT PROCESSING/STOREFRONT SERVICES

Amazon: https://amazon.com

PayPal: https://paypal.com

Shopify: http://www.shopify.com

ADVERTISING

Google AdSense: https://www.google.com/adsense/start

Media.net: http://www.media.net

MARKETING/SOCIAL MEDIA

Facebook: http://facebook.com

Instagram: http://instagram.com

MailChimp: http://mailchimp.com

Pinterest: http://pinterest.com

Share This plugin: https://wordpress.org/plugins/share-this

Twitter: http://twitter.com

INDEX

A

A/B testing, 96
Access control, 101–102
Add Media, 37
Ads
  selling, 74–75
  web-based, 97
Affiliate management, 72
Akismet, 40–42, 46, 82, 83
All in one SEO pack, 46
Amazon, 71
  Webstore, 72
Analytics package,
  picking, 93–95
API (Application
  Programming
  Interface), 41, 106
Audience profiles, 62, 96
Automattic, 28
Avatar, 83, 106

B

Backups, 104–105
Bidding, 60
Bing, 61
Blogger, being good, 68
Blogging, 66
Blogs, 11, 106
Boardshorts.com, 11, 13, 14
Bounce rate, 91
Brochure sites, 13, 18, 67,
  92, 106
Browser compatibility, 31
Business-card sites, 13, 106

C

Cashmore, Pete, 16
Categories, 51
Checkout page, 57
Cloud commerce, 72–73
Comment, creating and
  managing, 80–84
Comment spam, 82

Constant Content, 69
Contact form, 46
  creating, 84
Content
  buying, 69–70
  quality of, 68
Content creation, 63–65
  outsourcing of, 65
  rolling, 64–65
  users in, 66
Content Management
  System (CMS), 11, 106
Content mill, 69, 106
Conversion funnel, 95
Copyright issues, 69–70
Coupon options, 71

D

Dashboard
  administration, 103
Database, 104
Denial of Service (DoS), 102
Developer, 10, 27, 30, 31, 39,
  85, 86, 88, 101, 106
Developments, keeping up
  with new, 103

E

E-commerce sites, 18, 35,
  66, 67, 93
  steps in making, 76–77
Elance, 69
Exits, 92

F

Facebook, 97
Features, adding, 39
Ferriss, Tim, 15
Footer menu, 48
Forums, 66
The 4-Hour Chef, website
  for, 15
Friends, making, 85

G

General Public License, 27
Getty Images, 69
Ghost Bloggers, 69
Goals
  identifying your, 20–21
  setting your, 18–19
Google, 54, 61, 71
  AdSense plugin, 75
Google Analytics, 93–95
Google Webmaster Tools, 57
Google XML sitemaps, 46

H

Hosting provider, 106
Hosts, choosing, 27–29
HTML syntax, 61
Hybrids, 18

I

Interactive sites, 67, 92
Internet, power of the, 80
Intranet, 106
iStockphoto, 69

J

Jetpack, 46

K

Keywords, 54, 56, 60, 106
  geographical, 62
  selecting, 62

L

Layout, 34

M

MailChimp, 71
Marketing campaign, 71
Marketing site, 18, 67, 92
Mashable.com, 13, 16–17
Media files,
  managing, 44–45

Media Library, 44, 45, 47
Media sites, 18, 67, 93
Metrics
    selecting your, 90–93
    using, 95–96
Mobile menu, 47
Multisite, 15, 28, 107

O

Odesk, 69
Online reviews, 72
Online sales, 73–74
Open-source code, 27
Organized, getting, 47–51
Outsourcing of content
    creation, 65

P

Page menus,
    managing, 47–50
Pages, 36
Pages per session, 91
Page views, 91
Payment, 70–72
    calculation of, 71
PayPal, 71
Plagiarism, 69–70, 110
Plugins, 13, 39, 57, 58,
    96, 103
    patches for, 103
    playing with, 40–42
    popular, 46–47
Posts, 35, 36, 80
    tagging and
        categorizing, 50–51
Primary navigation, 47
Product inventory
    management, 71
Profiles, 55

Q

QR code, 97

R

Really Simple Syndication
    (RSS), 66
Reporting, 72
Robots.txt, 57

S

Screen Options menu, 103
Scripted, 69
Search engine optimization
    (SEO), 31, 53–57,
    61, 107
Security, 98–101
Servers, 28
Sessions, 91
Shopify, 72
Sitemap, 46, 57, 107
Small business, need for
    website, 8–10
SMART goals, 19, 90
Snoop Dogg, website of,
    11–12
Social media, 97, 107
    attracting traffic
        with, 58–60
Software integration, 71
Sources, 91
Spam, 107
Spammers, 80
Spiders, 57
Static pages, 35
Sub-pages, 35
Success, measuring
    your, 90–97
Sweden, website of, 14

T

Tags, 50–51
Taxonomy, 52
Templates, 70–71
Thank-you page, 57
Themes, 26–27, 103
    browser compatibility
        and, 31
    picking, 30–33
    search optimization
        and, 31
    speed and, 31
    support and, 31
Timelines, adjusting, 69
Titles, 54, 56, 61
Top-bar navigation, 48
Traffic, attracting, with
    social media, 58–60
Transaction handling, 71
Twenty Fifteen, 27

U

Updates, 68
URL structure, 61
Users, 91
    in content creation, 66

V

Visits, 91
Visual editor, 36
Vogue.com, 11

W

Web-based advertising, 97
Web crawlers, 57
Website, small business'
    need for, 8–10
Website architecture, 34–39
    about us, 35
    blog, 35
    contact us, 34, 35, 38
    news, 34
    privacy/terms of use, 35
    thank you, 35
Widgets, 39
    working with, 42–43
Woocommerce, 46
WordCamp, 88
WordPress
    advantages to, 28
    benefits of, 11
    drawbacks of, 28–29
    flexibility of, 11
    market share and, 11
    uses of, 15, 22–23
WordPress
    community, 88–90
WordPress forums, 86–88
WordPress license, 27

Y

Yahoo, 61
Yeager, Chuck, website of,
    11, 12

MAKE
THE INTERNET
YOUR ASSET

EARN MORE WITH

'NET WORTH

Guides

 TYCHO PRESS

Also available as eBooks

JEFFERSON COUNTY LIBRARY
620 Cedar Avenue
Port Hadlock, WA 98339
(360) 385-6544 www.jclibrary.info

CPSIA information can be obtained at www.ICGtesting.com
Printed in the USA
BVOW11s0023051115

425548BV00001B/1/P